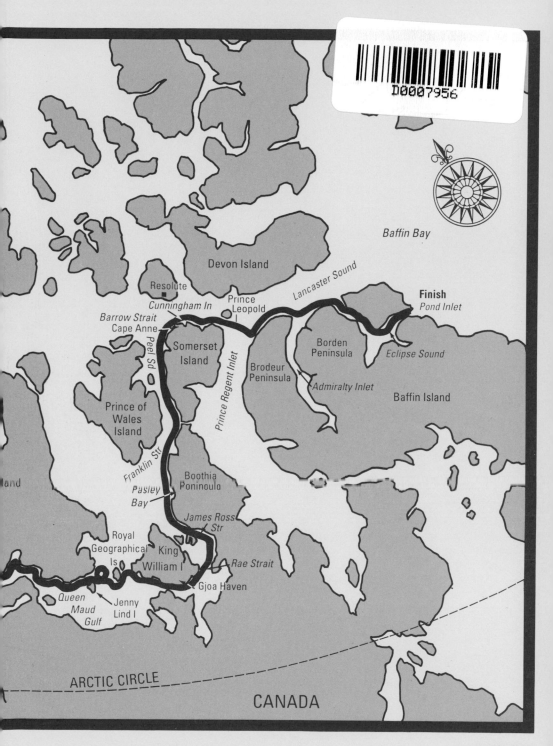

Baffin Bay

Devon Island

Resolute
Cunningham In
Prince
Leopold
I

Lancaster Sound

Finish
Pond Inlet

Barrow Strait
Cape Anne

Peel Sd

Somerset
Island

Borden
Peninsula

Eclipse Sound

Brodeur
Peninsula

Prince Regent Inlet

Prince of
Wales
Island

Admiralty Inlet

Baffin Island

Franklin Str

Boothia
Peninsula

Pasley
Bay

James Ross
Str

Royal
Geographical
Is

King
William I

Rae Strait

Gjoa Haven

*Queen
Maud
Gulf*

Jenny
Lind I

ARCTIC CIRCLE

CANADA

ArtPlus Ltd.

Polar Passage

THE HISTORIC FIRST SAIL THROUGH THE NORTHWEST PASSAGE

Polar Passage

THE
HISTORIC
FIRST SAIL
THROUGH
THE
NORTHWEST
PASSAGE

JEFF MacINNIS
WITH WADE ROWLAND

Random House
Toronto

Published in Canada by Random House of Canada Limited, Toronto.

Canadian Cataloguing in Publication Data

MacInnis, Jeff, 1963-
  Polar passage

Includes index.
ISBN 0-394-22083-8

1. MacInnis, Jeff, 1963-   . 2. Beedell,
Mike, 1956-   . 3. Northwest Passage.
I. Rowland, Wade, 1944-   . II. Title.

G650.1986.M33 1989   910'.09163'27   C89-093241-7

COVER DESIGN by Brant Cowie/Artplus Ltd.
COVER PHOTOGRAPHS by Mike Beedell
INSERT PHOTOGRAPHS by Mike Beedell and Jeff MacInnis

Printed in Canada

To all of those who made this dream a reality. Thank you for your support, spirit, and ideas.

Jeff MacInnis

Contents

Our team of supporters is extensive indeed. This group of people shared the dream of sailing the Northwest Passage and taught me more than they will ever realize. In particular, I wish to highlight a few of them: my father, who inspired and guided me; Mike Beedell, who journeyed with me so long and patiently; Cathy Stedman, whose spirit and efforts helped make it possible; Peter Jess, whose Arctic expertise helped solve many of our problems; my mother who has supported me in all my endeavours; and three of our strongest sponsors who personally shared our dream: Peter Widdrington of Labatt's; Doug Campbell of Hobie Cat; and Norman James of the Canadian National Sportsmen Show. I wish also to thank the team that helped put this book together: Wade Rowland, who crafted my extensive journals into this book; Jack McClelland, who acted as my agent; and the group at Random House of Canada, including Ed Carson, Doug Pepper, Pat Cairns, and Susan Meisner.

The following sponsors and supporters have also contributed greatly to the Polar Passage Expedition:

John Labatt Ltd., Canadian National Sportsmen Shows, Hobie Cat, Alpha Graphics Ltd., Baker Marine, Bomac Batten, Bushnell, Business Theatres, Chlorophylle Ltd., Coleman Company, Catamarine, Davidson Chrysler Dodge, Diving Unlimited International, E-Z Loader, Expert, W.L. Gore & Associates, Grift-Grabbers, Harken, Helm Designs, Hot Chillys, Hot Fingers, Jessco, Motorola, Murrays Marine, Nike, North Sailing Products, Olympus, Panasonic, Primedia, Pro-Cam, Random House of Canada Ltd., Rocky Mountain Cycle, Rolex, Saffer Advertising Inc., Sierra Designs, Sony, Tilley Endurables, 3M Canada, University of Western Ontario, George Weston Ltd.

Peter Alford, Wayne Anderson, Susan Aziz, Jack Baker, Kathy Barclay, Mike Beckerman, Peter Bigny, John Bleasby, John Bockstoce, David Bristow, George Brooks, Bob Brown, Al Chandler, Joe Charlesworth, Damir Chytil, Gilles Couet, David Couper, John Cowan, Bob Cranston, Rob Crowder, Bill Curtsinger, Jacquie Czerv, Roger Davidson, Ed Dayholos, Ken Dudley, Mike Dukelow, Bob Engle, Blake Farrow, Craig Farrow, David Fergusson, Howard Fergusson, Pat Ferns, Dr. Fitzjames, Geoff Genovese, Greg Glista, Jim Godden, Bill Graves, Richard Gulland, Dr. Peter Hanson, Mr. Hardy, Helen Hare, Donna Harris, Jonathan Harris, Bonnie Hepburn, David Hill, George Hobson, Barry Huff, Peter Hughes, Jack Hurst, Doug Irwin, Darren Jack, Ted Janulis, Judy Jess, Pete Jess, C.B. Johnston, Frank Joinman, Brian Jones, Barbara Kincaid, Gary King, Cheryl Knapp, Emory Kristof, Kim Kymlicka, John Lacato, Tracy Lacato, Paul Lang, Willie Laserich, David Leighton, Martin Lilley, Roger Lindsey, Merv Little, Dick Long, Rob Luske, Bill Lyall, John Lynn, Debbie MacInnis, Janet MacInnis, Jordan MacInnis, Lara MacInnis, Moby MacInnis, the Manchees, Bill Mason, Ray Masygen, Peter McConville, Shawn McConville, Stew McDonald, Gary McGuffin, Joanie McGuffin, Bill McIntosh, Bruce McKelfrish, Denise Mckenzie, Harland Molen, Keith Moorehead, Dave Mudry, Steve Murray, the Nellas, David Nettelship, Valerie Nogas, Phil Nuytten, Dr. Pedersen, Mark Precious, Jackie Radley, Brian Reesor, Neil Remmie, Ms. Ridley, Phil Riggs, Victor Royce, Gary Rubanoff, David Saffer, Doreen Sanders, Michael Sanderson, Schuyler Sanderson, Mr. S.A. Sauer, Walley Schaber, Robert Schad, John Schuch, Dan Scinocca, Christine Shumsky, Astel Singer, Laurie Skreslet, Bruce Smith, Ross Smith, Tom Smith, Tonia Smithers, Helmut Siepman, Bob Stinton, Ian Sullivan, Ernie Thomas, Alex Tilley, Betty Ann VanGastel, Paul Ullibarri, Ian Varte, Margaret Wahl, John Wake, Barbara Warnik, Dan Webster, John Welton, Ralph White, Robert Williams, Mr. D.G. Willox, Miles Wood, Mary Wright, Paul Zemla.   Thank you.

Prologue

Like most journeys, mine began with a dream, then the hard slogging of planning, testing and preparation — in this case, three long years of it. It was a process filled with a thousand and one intricate details, but to call it humdrum or tedious would be misleading. Because, as each question was clarified and answered, as each piece of equipment was evaluated and selected, as each of the hundreds of potential problems was identified and dealt with, I was coming closer to the realization of my goal. And the challenge I was dealing with could scarcely have been more exciting: to organize an expedition that would make the first-ever unassisted sail-powered transit of the infamous Northwest Passage. Many great explorers had faced the same challenge during the golden age of maritime exploration when Britannia ruled the waves and her ships were charting undiscovered passages in the remotest corners of the globe. Yet the Northwest Passage defeated them, and at a

1

terrible cost. In their agony and frustration, they called it an ice-choked hell.

For three years I saw myself as a collector of ideas, communicating with scores of experts in every aspect of Arctic survival and logistics, fitting bits of advice into a multidimensional puzzle in which the integrity of the whole depended on the utility of each of the individual pieces. The selection of so simple a piece of equipment as a paddle became a complex question when it was realized that it would have to serve several purposes: as a tool to propel our boat through the water when there was no wind, of course, but also as a shovel for cutting snow blocks for windbreaks, as a mast for a radio antenna, as a boat hook for catching lines and fending off ice.

In this sense, each choice involved a life-and-death decision, for we would be sailing in as harsh a marine environment as exists anywhere in the world, where heaving, grinding ice, numbing water and wildly erratic weather mix in challenging and potentially deadly combinations. It could not help but be an endlessly fascinating process.

All along the torturously winding route of the plan's evolution, I called on the advice and support of many people, but no one more than my father, Dr. Joe MacInnis, who knew the Arctic intimately and in particular knew its waters and the dangers they held. As leader of, and participant in, fifteen expeditions throughout Canada's north, he had made hundreds of lonely and often dangerous journeys under the ice, exploring techniques for diving in the polar environment and studying the effects of that environment on man.

He had been an explorer in a more conventional sense as well, searching out and probing the most northerly shipwreck on the planet. It had been watching him in this role, as leader of an expedition to find and photograph the nineteenth-century

Royal Navy bark *Breadalbane*, that had inspired me to want to
lead an Arctic expedition of my own.

It was in April 1983, and I had come to the Arctic with my
father almost immediately after completing an intensely
frustrating season in Europe with the Canadian National Ski
Team. Snow conditions had been impossible until well after
Christmas and the team, myself included, did badly. One of my
closest friends on the team crashed horribly during a training
run in Morzine, France, on a course that should have been
closed, given the deplorable conditions. He was lifted off the
course in a helicopter, his femur broken, his racing days over
forever, while the organizers called in the next contestant. As
members of this elite team, we were constantly being pitted
against one another to qualify to represent the country in races.
Egos grew inflamed or were crushed; we were out for blood.

By the end of that season I had begun to doubt whether I
really wanted to be involved in this type of sport. As much as
I loved it and loved the competition, in my experience it seemed
to deny rather than affirm the best of the participants' human
instincts. It was a fine example of motivation by intimidation
rather than inspiration.

The *Breadalbane* expedition was an awakening. I watched
my father calmly and effectively coordinate a team of the
world's foremost experts in underwater research, always
weighing his words carefully before speaking, cheerfully
undertaking the most menial tasks in working toward the
success of the venture. In the incredibly harsh environment of
the ice off Beechey Island, far north of the Arctic Circle, I
watched the creative interaction among men like National
Geographic's Emory Kristof, the world's foremost deep-
water photographer; Phil Nuytten, president and founder
of one of the world's most successful commercial diving
companies, CanDive of Vancouver, and this expedition's

diving coordinator; and Peter Jess of Jessco, logistics specialist and ice expert on loan from Dome Petroleum, the expedition's problem solver.

Each of these men was a giant in his field, and yet their individual egos seemed to meld, rather than clash. They were a team in a way in which the National Ski Team was not. I began to see that this was the way great things ought to be accomplished – in a spirit of harmony, rather than conflict. However, I was to discover that it is a skill not easily learned.

Though none could sail with me on my tiny vessel, each of these men was on my team, having provided the advice and support and inspiration that made the expedition possible and ensured its ultimate success.

There were others. Miles Wood is an experienced catamaran ocean racer who convinced me that weight was the most critical factor in our planning, that too much weight would not only slow the boat and make it difficult to maneuver, but would make it almost impossible to right after a capsize. He also provided many valuable tips on storing provisions and rigging the vessel for extreme conditions. Most of all, he gave me invaluable coaching on how to sail the uniquely fleet-winged and maneuverable boat that is the Hobie 18. Given the fact that I took delivery of my boat from the factory just twelve months before the expedition began – and until that time had had little sailing experience of any kind – his support was crucial. Dick Long, the president of Diving Unlimited International of San Diego, California, constructed the high-tech Gore-Tex waterproof diving suits that would make it possible for us to survive in the sub-zero Arctic environment. There were many others, team players all.

One day just weeks before I was to depart for the north, the planning almost complete, the sponsors in place and the equipment on order or delivered, my father took me aside after a family dinner.

"I want to tell you a story," he said, and I knew it was something serious. "This has to be between you and me, because I don't want anybody else to know how concerned I am. But you *must* know.

"Three of the sea people I've known best have lost children to the ocean. Three of them. When you know these people and see their suffering it affects you. And I can't help wondering sometimes if there's a kind of fate at work in all of this, that the sons of sea people are particularly at risk."

The three men, he said, were Edwin Link, Jacques Cousteau and Mel Fisher. Link had been my father's mentor, a man who had turned his wealth and talent as designer of the Link pilot trainer to developing the equipment divers would need to probe deep into the undersea world. In 1973 his son Clay had met a terrible end, freezing to death in a submersible snared by the wreck of a ship in the deep waters off Florida.

"I was there the next day," my father said. "I saw Ed just crying and crying. I saw my hero utterly devastated. It was shattering."

Philippe Cousteau, son of Jacques, the "grand seigneur" of diving, the light of his father's life, had been a special friend of my father's. Philippe had died in the crash of the Cousteau flying boat in 1979. Again, my father said, the loss had been traumatic.

"He was the spirit of Calypso. He was the guy who was supposed to inherit the Cousteau mantle. Nobody could believe he'd died that way."

And finally, there had been Mel Fisher, an American folk hero, discoverer of a fabulously rich wreck of a Spanish galleon who for sixteen years had fought the elements and the U.S. government to salvage the $350 million treasure. Each morning he would say, "Today's the day!"

One night in 1975 the dive ship lying over the wreck suddenly and inexplicably turned turtle, drowning Fisher's son, his daughter-in-law and another diver. One more golden son taken by the sea.

"Maybe," my father said, "there's a reason why all three of these people died. Maybe it was because they grew up with the ocean like you have, sons of sea people, and maybe because of that they didn't respect her the way they should have. Maybe they didn't understand what a vicious lady she can be when she wants to.

"I don't know if it's possible to really understand how quickly the Arctic can kill you until you've felt your skull go numb in the water or seen the ice closing over your head in a dive hole, or been around when a storm blows up so quickly it makes the hair stand up on the back of your neck. You must — *must* — learn to fear her more than you do."

My father has an expression he uses sometimes, "the old gray wolf knocking at your door." In those moments, I felt its breath and smelled its pungent odor. In the night I dreamed about a many-roomed mansion on a hill, brooding, haunted, but exerting an irresistible attraction.

A door had been opened before me and a chill wind blew through it, but it could not be closed. Beyond it were truths I had yet to discover, truths that transcended the journey, truths about life, and the nearness of death, that were as hard and cold and immutable as the polar ice.

YEAR ONE — 1986

July 20 – August 29

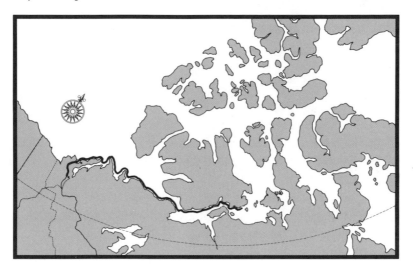

Chapter 1

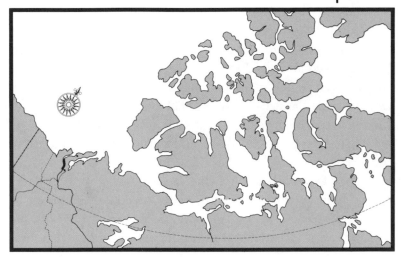

It was 3 A.M. on a frosty morning in late July, and the sun was very low on the horizon when the big Hughes 212 helicopter clawed its way into the air and clattered out over Barrow Strait.

As we swept south, the ice cover beneath us increased steadily until by the time we'd reached Peel Sound, there was no open water to be seen in any direction. No open water, and yet we were expecting to sail through this historic passage in just a few weeks.

The pilot's voice crackled in my headset over the din of the engine. "I'd say it's about six feet thick down there right now. You guys might as well head right on home. There's not a hope in hell of getting through that stuff."

I didn't respond — there was nothing I could say. I knew from studying years of ice maps that it was still too early in the summer to expect much open water, that the warmth of July normally melts and weakens the ice enough for it to break up through August and early September, when freeze-up begins again. Even so, I had not expected this kind of continuous ice cover this late in the season.

The rest of our flight from the high Arctic supply depot of Resolute Bay south and west 2000 km to Inuvik near the rim of the Beaufort Sea was no more encouraging. All along the route that we hoped to sail, the sea was still locked in ice that looked like a cracked and weathered coat of stucco, and which I knew was as often as not an almost impenetrable jumble of broken, rafted shards the size of boxcars. The only navigable waters in the whole route were a 130-km stretch of Beaufort Sea coastline leading east from Tuktoyaktuk, and the waters at the mouth of the Mackenzie River.

I looked behind me at Mike Beedell, who three months earlier had signed on to accompany me on the journey as expedition photographer. As usual, he was occupied with his cameras, an artist watching out the Plexiglas window for a shot. Mike had a great deal of Arctic experience and I knew that he must be worried too, though it would be unlike him to show much concern.

We had heard that it was a bad summer for ice, but this was worse than bad. This was disastrous. We had come so far and worked so hard and planned so long and accepted so many favors (including this helicopter reconnaissance flight) from people who believed in us, and now it looked as though we were beaten before we'd begun. I felt like a condemned man on a forced march to the scaffold. There was no turning back.

I was beginning to think that we were in over our heads. Mike and I were trying to win where so many of the great explorers of the past had lost. The Arctic's deadly and mysterious aura had attracted men of the highest caliber, from Martin Frobisher, Henry Hudson, Robert Bylot and the rest of the amazing Elizabethans, to the indomitable Victorians — Franklin, Ross, Rae, McClure and a host of others. Despite four centuries of effort, no one had yet succeeded in sailing the passage. Captain James Cook, perhaps the greatest navigator of all, had declared flatly that no one ever would.

There were of course very good reasons for this. The Northwest Passage is the most difficult maritime route in the world. Parts of it are 800 km north of the Arctic Circle, and for nine months of the year its entire 3500-km length is locked in ice. Even during the brief six- to twelve-week summer, half the passage is infested with enough ice to make navigation difficult in most years, impossible in the rest. In winter, the sun disappears below the horizon, winds rise to hurricane force and temperatures can drop as low as $-50°C$. What visibility the darkness affords is often obscured by blizzards and white-outs. In summer, fog is a constant problem. Magnetic compasses are useless for most of the passage because of the proximity of the magnetic pole, and modern electronic aids to navigation are often plagued by interference.

Time and again, for four centuries and more, explorers seeking a polar route to the Orient were rebuffed when their vessels were seized in the ice and held tight. Ships would lie enchained sometimes for years on end, while their crews succumbed one by one to the fatal agonies of scurvy, starvation, frostbite and madness.

Even with the advent of modern steam, gasoline and diesel power, the passage had been negotiated just a handful of times, and then, with two exceptions, only by steel ships specially built for Arctic travel with reinforced icebreaking prows and enormously powerful engines. The first exception was the wooden sloop *Gjoa*, in which Norwegian Roald Amundsen and a crew of six became the first men to complete the passage, motor-sailing from east to west in the three years from 1903 to 1906. The *Gjoa*, a refitted fishing boat of more than thirty years' experience in the North Atlantic, was 22 m long and displaced

47 tonnes. For much of the voyage, she relied for motive power on a 13-horsepower gasoline engine. Later, Amundsen became the first person to reach the South Pole.

The other exception was the Royal Canadian Mounted Police auxiliary schooner *St. Roch*, which was the second vessel to complete the passage, the first to do it from west to east, and the first to navigate it both ways. Leaving Vancouver in June 1940 under the command of RCMP Sergeant Henry Larsen, the *St. Roch* first made the transit from west to east wintering in the Arctic archipelago, as had Amundsen. In 1944 the doughty little ship traveled the return route in only eighty-six days.

The *St. Roch* was 31 m long and built of Douglas fir sheeted over with Australian gumwood or ironbark, a very hard wood that could withstand the grinding of ice. Her main engine on the first passage was a 150-horsepower diesel, but that was upgraded to a 300-horsepower model for the east-west journey. She had accommodations for thirteen officers and men.

By contrast, the first commercial vessel to negotiate the passage, the American experimental icebreaking tanker *S.S. Manhattan*, displaced 138,000 tonnes and was as long as the Empire State Building is high. Her icebreaking bow alone weighed 725 tonnes and she was girdled with a 2000-tonne steel ice belt, 5 m high. (Despite this armor, ice tore a 5 by 8 m hole in one of her forward tanks.) She made it through the passage in about two weeks in September 1969, at times smashing through 5-m thicknesses of ice. But she made it only by the skin of her teeth and only with the constant assistance of the Canadian icebreaker *John A. Macdonald*. Her builders estimated that ships used in regular commercial traffic through the passage would have to be twice the size of the *Manhattan*.

The route followed by the *Manhattan* and her consort, *John A. Macdonald*, took her through Lancaster Sound and then on to Viscount Melville Sound to the north of Victoria Island. She tried to punch her way into the Beaufort Sea through ice-choked M'Clure Strait but was very nearly trapped. The ship escaped only with the assistance of the Canadian icebreaker and by diverting steam from the cabin heating system to her engine boilers to squeeze out a few extra horsepower. She then dodged south to freedom and the Beaufort Sea through the Prince of Wales Strait.

Amundsen had followed a more southerly route, entering the passage via Lancaster Sound but then steering south down Peel Sound, looping south of King William Island and on to the south of Victoria Island and Banks Island.

The *St. Roch* traced Amundsen's route for most of its west-to-east passage, slipping through Bellot Strait into Prince Regent Inlet to avoid the notorious ice blockade in Peel Sound. On her return journey, she'd pioneered the northerly route that would be taken by the *Manhattan* and succeeded in negotiating M'Clure Strait where the larger ship was to be turned back.

It was Amundsen's route that I had chosen to follow, tracing it in reverse, from west to east. The vessel I had selected took to its logical conclusion Amundsen's philosophy that, in the Arctic, small is better. We would be sailing a 5.5-m Hobie catamaran that weighed just 280 kg fully laden, provided no shelter for its crew, and had only minimal storage capacity in its twin fiberglass hulls. We would compensate for her lack of shelter by providing ourselves with the best survival gear we could find, including dry-suits and full flotation coveralls, and when possible, we would sleep ashore in a mountaineering tent.

In return for the constant exposure to the elements our boat imposed on her crew, the Hobie cat would offer several advantages over conventional craft. She was very fast even in light airs and small enough to be paddled, albeit slowly, when there was no wind at all. The Hobie cat was light enough to be hauled up on shore out of harm's way in a storm, and sturdy enough to be dragged over ice for short distances in the event we encountered impenetrable barriers separating us from open water. Though her storage capacity was limited, there was enough space in her hulls and on her canvas "deck" to carry our essential equipment and provisions for a little over three weeks.

I named her *Perception*, and before she left the factory the bottoms of her bright yellow hulls had been reinforced with thin strips of bullet-proof Kevlar plastic, which I hoped would make her impervious to holing by ice when sailing. To protect her and to ease her way when she was being hauled over rough ice, we'd made a set of thin plastic runners, which strapped onto the banana-shaped hulls like a hockey player's shin pads. Later, out of necessity, we would add an old pair of my Fischer downhill skis to her inventory, for use on those rare occasions when we encountered stretches of relatively smooth ice. I'd learned to sail the Hobie in the Great Lakes, in the rolling Gulf Stream seas off Florida, and finally in the ice-choked waters of Georgian Bay on Lake Huron, where I'd performed cold weather trials for boat and survival gear.

Along with the technical side of the voyage, there was the equally complicated business side to contend with. The initial feasibility studies for the Polar Passage Expedition were done as part of my studies in 1985 to 1986 at the University of Western Ontario's School of Business Administration. During my second year there, I'd had a problem: time. Trying to get the Polar Passage expedition off the ground and at the same time keeping up with my course work was more than I could handle. The solution was to persuade my professors that Polar Passage met the criteria for the business feasibility study that students were required to complete that year. This took some doing, since the professors were mainly used to examining proposals for new consumer products and house-painting companies. An expedition, especially one in remote regions of the Arctic, seemed too strange and glamorous to merit consideration. In the end, though, they accepted my argument that to succeed in any expedition, however exotic, one must first build on a sound business foundation.

I soon formed a team with four classmates — Cathy Stedman, Susan Manchee, Margaret Wahl and Joe Charlesworth — and we worked hard to assemble a solid business plan for sailing the passage with 100 percent business sponsorship. Our plan covered fifty pages of analysis and recommendations, including a point-by-point strategy for reaching the expedition's financial goals. Not only was the document an invaluable asset in meetings with potential sponsors, it earned our business team first place in the 3000-student competition.

The yearning for Arctic adventure had been part of me for a long time. I was ten years old when I first traveled to the north in 1973 to join my father on Baffin Island, where he was trying to film beluga whales underwater. It would be difficult to imagine a more exciting event in a young child's life — it seemed like a trip to Mars. Two years later I was back, being as helpful as I could while Dad worked on the film *And the Narwhals Came*. In 1978, 1980 and 1983 I joined my father in the successful search for the British ship *Breadalbane*, sunk in 1853 off Beechey Island while it was assisting in the search for the doomed Franklin expedition.

The magnetic tug of the north seeped quickly into my veins, and while I treasured the experiences I'd had with my father, I felt a growing need to do something special, something unique that would allow me to claim the Arctic in my own way.

"Something special" took a long time to define. It had to be an adventure with a purpose. And it had to be in harmony with my inner growth. I had spent much of my adolescence single-mindedly preparing myself to be a world caliber downhill ski racer at the international level and I hoped this Arctic journey would enable me to harness in a constructive way the competitive instincts I had so assiduously honed on the ski slopes. As to its purpose, I believe, as do most who know the Arctic, that it is vital to the Canadian identity to understand and embrace its awesome splendors. I hoped our journey would make Canadians more aware of their northern frontier and the wonderful gifts that lie therein, largely undiscovered and unappreciated. I also feel strongly that the waters of the passage are, and must remain, Canadian. This would be our chance to make a small statement about Canadian sovereignty.

The three long and trying years of intensive planning ended and the journey began on July 1, 1986 — Canada Day. *Perception* had been stripped down, wrapped in heavy-gauge cardboard and plastic sheeting, then lashed securely to her trailer in readiness for the 10,000-km journey west across Canada and north beyond the Arctic Circle to the end of the road at Inuvik. Mike Beedell was already in the north on a photographic expedition to Pangnirtung on Baffin Island and planned to meet me at Resolute in time for the helicopter reconnaissance we'd planned. Cathy Stedman would be my copilot on the long road ahead.

As I carefully drove the heavily laden Dodge Caravan down the driveway of our Toronto home and into the street, the trailer hitch ground into the sidewalk with a nerve-wrenching squeal. We were overloaded, no doubt about it: the past weeks had been chaos trying to get everything packed and organized. Even the seagoing kayak we'd strapped to the roof was stuffed to the gills.

Five days later we rolled into Calgary, where we were to spend the night at the home of Peter and Judy Jess. Pete had already given me much good advice on how to equip the expedition, and now I wanted to talk over the plan with him one more time and make final arrangements for the Resolute to Inuvik helicopter flight he'd managed to squeeze us aboard. Before we left the city, we purchased the shotgun that would be our defence of last resort against grizzly and polar bears. We also bought the aircraft and high-frequency radios we would use to keep in contact with the outside world.

We drove fifteen hours a day, camping each night, from Calgary to Edmonton to Whitehorse in the Yukon. From there a long, dusty, bone-rattling ride took us toward Dawson and the beginning of the Dempster Highway, the continent's northernmost all-weather road. With 1100 km of gravel ahead and only one gas station along the way, we filled up the two plastic jerry cans we'd brought and struck out north for Inuvik, where our long sea journey would begin.

Chapter 2

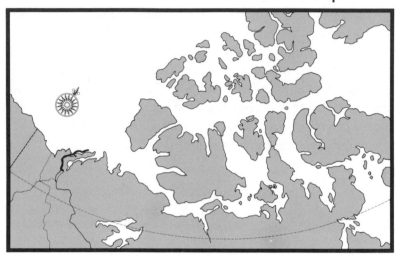

Hordes of bloodthirsty blackflies tried mightily, but failed to prevent us from getting a good night's rest at our Inuvik campsite following our eighteen-hour helicopter ride from Resolute. The sleep helped to restore my confidence somewhat and Mike, Cathy and I enthusiastically set about the task of assembling *Perception* and loading her with supplies and equipment.

We had lightened her burden to some extent by storing some of our provisions in the 6-m plastic kayak we planned to tow. But when we launched the fully laden boat, she still floated alarmingly low in the water, and with the kayak in tow we had a great deal of difficulty tacking in light winds. Nevertheless, at 8 P.M. on the evening of July 20, 1986, Mike and I waved goodby to a small group of well-wishers, including my mother, Cathy and several friends we'd made in Inuvik. We were finally off, as I steered *Perception*'s twin bows down the silt-laden Mackenzie

River in the direction of the Beaufort Sea about 130 km to the north.

I had expected the sail down the Mackenzie on the breast of a three-knot current to be relatively easy going, but the wind was right on our nose out of the north and to make any progress, we had to wrestle the boat back and forth across the river, tack after difficult tack. A steady rain didn't make it any more pleasant.

We sailed for five hours before we spotted a clutch of tents in the lee of the grassy Caribou Hills; we pulled in wet and cold at the Inuit camp, where an elderly woman greeted us and plied us with hot tea. Winnie's toothless smile and weathered face reflected the harsh environment we had entered, and the generosity of her welcome in the small hours of the morning provided our first taste of the warm northern hospitality we would enjoy throughout our voyage.

Our headwind persisted through the following day, as did the rain. My prototype waterproof sailing suit was already leaking in several places. It was too small for me, as well, which made it difficult to bend every time the mainsail boom swung overhead for a tack. The river was the color of chocolate milk and so shallow that we ran aground scores of times while trying to find our way through the confusing maze of channels in the winding delta. That night we camped right on the riverbank, climbing wearily into our mountaineering bivouac sacks without bothering to erect the tent.

Early in the morning Mike spotted the tents of an Inuit hunting camp on the west shore of the shallow river channel we were zigzagging through. Since our progress was negligible thanks to nearly nonexistent winds, we decided to say hello. Two young children met us at the beach as we splashed ashore and they took us to where their father was working. The family had recently killed a beluga whale and strips of blubber and

meat were being hung out on racks to dry. A charnel-house
stench of blood and raw flesh filled the air and seemed to attract
every mosquito for miles around. We chatted and took
photographs until a freshening breeze beckoned us back to
Perception and the river.

The wind, though stronger, was once again from the north
and now that our channel had widened, the river was getting
quite choppy. Each time we tacked, water washed over the
coated fabric trampoline that decked the area between the twin
hulls of our overburdened vessel. If it was this wet in a sheltered
river channel, I wondered how we would survive on the open
ocean.

Off in the distance, we could see the river delta fanning out
into the sea. A series of white navigation markers came into
view, which we found difficult to follow given the direction of
the wind and *Perception*'s clumsy handling. But we quickly
learned that it was essential to stay within the channel when one
of the boat's dagger boards struck bottom, stopping us as
though we'd been jerked back on a leash and pitching the vessel
up on its leeward hull. I released the mainsheet instantly to
reduce the pressure of wind on the mainsail, but for a long, long
second, it seemed that we were going to either break the board
in half or flip right over. Slowly, she settled back, and we
proceeded more cautiously.

As we left the protection of the river and sailed north and east
under freshening winds into Kugmallit Bay, we began
encountering large ocean swells that eventually forced us
ashore for the night on a barren spit of land. We pitched our
tent amongst the rocks and a litter of seal vertebrae left behind
by generations of native hunters.

We had entered the land of pingos, ice-cored hills that thrust
themselves up out of the permafrost under the pressure of
freezing ground water in dry lake or river beds. These
cone-shaped oddities can grow to be as high as 50 m, in their

initial stages rising up by as much as half a meter a year. Clothed in tundra vegetation of tawny grass, dwarf willow and sedge, their cores are solid blue ice, which often breaks through at the peaks and melts, leaving the pingos looking like miniature volcanoes. We could see dozens of them off to the east of us, the oldest of which we knew had been born more than a thousand years ago.

By early afternoon the next day, we were within sight of Tuktoyaktuk, but our progress remained agonizingly slow. The shallows along the shoreline forced us out into deeper waters, where the waves were high enough to bring *Perception* to a virtual standstill as her overweight bows plunged into the seas and threw up curtains of spray. We finally entered the harbor on July 23, three days — twenty-seven hours of sailing — out of Inuvik.

The rocky beach was populated by the stained and weather-beaten canvas tents of Inuit families summering here, and beyond that was a helter-skelter collection of a few dozen small frame houses on low permafrost stilts. The dominant architectural feature of the town was the huge radar dome of the DEW (Distant Early Warning) Line station. As the main supply center for the oil-drilling operations in the western Arctic, Tuk had at one time been a bustling community. With the drop in world oil prices, it had reverted to a quiet, cluttered backwater.

In Tuk we got down to the difficult process of going through our equipment and supplies and deciding what we could reasonably dispense with in order to lighten our vessel. First, we jettisoned our experimental waterproof sailing suits, which clearly needed more development before they'd be appropriate for the kind of conditions we'd be facing. We replaced them with DUI (Diving Unlimited International) suits that had been made for the U.S. navy to protect paratroops in ocean landings. They were made from a breathable Gore-Tex fabric and were totally watertight yet allowed perspiration vapor to escape. Their effectiveness in keeping us relatively warm and dry would be crucial to the success of the voyage. The minor problems Mike and I were to have with the suits were due mainly to the abuse from the razor-sharp ice they had to withstand.

We spread out our gear on the beach and began to make a pile of extra clothing, extra food, nonessential camera gear, extra stove fuel and other odds and ends. This operation reduced our margin of safety, but there was no way around it if we expected the boat to handle the rigors of ocean travel. We were slowly able to eliminate nearly 30 kg of gear, much of it food in excess of what we thought we'd need to reach Cambridge Bay, 1400 km to the east. By re-sorting the remaining equipment, we were able to dispense entirely with one of the three blue plastic barrels we'd lashed to the wings near the stern of the boat.

The Inuit kids living with their families on the beach were very curious about our equipment and were especially fascinated by our seagoing kayak. It was equipped with radio, food and a tent to serve as a lifeboat in case *Perception* was irreparably damaged at sea, and would provide a platform from which Mike could take photographs of the catamaran under sail. What we'd mainly used it for so far, though, was a kind of floating icebox; we'd placed our supplies of cheese and salami on the bottom of its hull. I had long since begun to wonder if we'd made a mistake in bringing it at all, but the kids had no doubts; they literally lined up for the chance to go out for a paddle. One young boy ran off down the beach still wearing my life jacket after a short ride. He returned a while later cradling an enormous, freshly gutted white fish in his arms. It was his way of thanking Mike and me, and we appreciated it, except that my jacket was now drenched in fish blood, a potent bear attractant. As quickly as I could I took the fish, thanked the smiling boy, helped him remove my life jacket and ran down to the sea to wash away the blood. The last thing I wanted was to smell like a polar bear's lunch for the next month.

There were two yachts in Tuk: one, the purposeful 15-m French staysail ketch *Vagabond II*, was anchored out in the harbor. Tied up at the government wharf was an elegant vessel that looked out of place in her rough-and-ready surroundings. She was the *Belvedere* out of New Bedford, Massachusetts, a sleek, 20-m, steel-hulled, pilot-house motor-sailer. Her owner, John Bockstoce, was an archaeologist and Arctic expert whose northern exploits had been featured in *National Geographic* along with my father's at the time of the *Breadalbane* discovery.

John invited us into his comfortable cabin. He uncorked a bottle of wine while Mike and I examined his extensive library of Arctic literature and looked in awe at the formidable array of navigation aids in the well-heated wheelhouse: there were several kinds of radios, a satellite navigation receiver, weather and ice facsimile machines, radar and more. We'd learned weeks before that John would be trying to navigate the Northwest Passage this year, and now he told us that *Vagabond II* would also be trying to force the passage this year.

Seeing up close the size and sophistication of *Belvedere* compared to our own little craft severely shook my confidence. Judging from her array of antennas, *Vagabond* appeared to be similarly equipped, though we weren't invited aboard. Her master left us with the impression that he didn't think much of our chances for success, though his crewmen seemed friendly enough.

We talked with John for an hour or more about our respective plans and he offered several pieces of sound advice, one of which I was to have cause to remember, too late, a few weeks later.

"Up here the weather can change so fast it'd make your head swim. Never, ever, leave your boat alone under any circumstances."

By July 27, we were trimmed down and as ready to meet whatever awaited us as we'd ever be. Though still unusually severe for this late in the season, ice conditions along our route were showing some small signs of improvement, according to the forecasts we received from Dome Petroleum's experts.

It was time to go. The first day of our adventure was underway. We had the first of our daily 8 A.M. radio schedules with Jim Godden at the federal government's Polar Continental Shelf Project headquarters in Tuk, which would monitor our progress and coordinate a rescue attempt should we fail to contact them in any seventy-two-hour period. That afternoon we lunched with Mike's friend Andy, an Anglican minister. He told us he would pray for a safe voyage.

We waited until early afternoon for a real wind to develop but it never did, and so at 4 P.M. we left Tuk harbor with only a teasing feeble breeze. It wasn't enough to fight the incoming tide, so we unshipped the paddles and got busy.

As we passed the DEW Line station, a worker ran down to the beach with his camera.

"Nobody down south will believe this without a picture," he yelled.

We had just passed through the channel markers at the harbor entrance when *Belvedere* motored by and turned her graceful prow due north. We exchanged waves. She was a magnificient boat, but at my age I wouldn't have traded places — facing the elements aboard *Perception* was more my idea of adventure.

The wind piped up once we were out on the open water and we had a splendid sail riding the trapeze through a moderate swell up the coast of the Tuktoyaktuk Peninsula. *Perception* was handling more like her old self.

The waters close to shore were still dangerously shallow, thanks to the build-up of silt from the Mackenzie River, and we touched bottom several times without, fortunately, doing any real damage. In one grounding, the line from which we were towing the kayak came loose and we had to turn back to retrieve the little boat. It was 1 A.M. when cold and fatigue finally forced us to stop and set up camp.

We awoke at 8:00 for our radio schedule, feeling decidedly the worse for wear; the sound of rain rattling the tent fly didn't help. In trying to get the HF radio antenna to work we got thoroughly soaked by the icy downpour. This was to be a problem throughout the voyage; the antenna consisted of 20 m of wire, which had to be stretched out between our paddles and oriented broadside to the station we wished to contact. We soon learned to set this up at night before retiring so we wouldn't have to do it in the morning, but it often blew down, and just as often our signal proved too weak to get through to Polar Shelf.

On this day we did eventually get through to report our position, but the wind was dead calm and so we climbed back into our sleeping bags for a few hours more rest. Just after noon, we made a huge breakfast of powdered eggs and freeze-dried beef stew but it wasn't until nearly 4:00 that there was enough wind to make it worthwhile launching our boat.

We saw our first whales shortly after we were underway — two white belugas almost as long as *Perception*, heading east at a speed we couldn't touch. And then the clammy, bone-chilling fog that is the bane of Arctic navigators rolled in on us, making it difficult to maintain contact with the shoreline and still stay in water deep enough to avoid grounding. The air temperature had been 10°C when we'd set out that day; when we pitched our tent for the night on the lee side of a sand spit, it was just above freezing at 1°C.

As I flipped to a clean page in my diary that night, I saw that

Cathy had written a personal note to me there, knowing I would find it a few days after she'd headed south from Inuvik with the van. It ended with a caution that indicated she knew me better, perhaps, than I did myself at that early stage in the journey: "To come this far with a dream is beautiful; to complete it would be magic. But nature must be ridden, not driven." It would be some time before I would learn to take those words to heart.

Dense fog, rain and a lack of wind delayed our start until late afternoon again the next day. Off Atkinson Point, we encountered our first ice. From our vantage point just a meter or two above the water, it looked as if we'd encountered solid pack ice, but as we got closer we could see that it was only a thin necklace of pans and floes strung across our path. We sailed in toward shore where the ice had grounded on the tide. We dragged *Perception* over the barrier and into open water on the other side.

The fog had embraced us once again as we groped our way along the coastline into McKinley Bay. Somewhere off to the left we could hear the muffled murmur of diesel engines, which we knew must be the generators at the Dome Petroleum offshore oil drilling operation nearby. We had an invitation to stop and enjoy a hot meal there, but more important than food was the problem with our radio. It didn't seem to be working properly and unless we could fix it or replace it, we would have to return to Tuk. So we changed our tack and steered toward the motors.

We paddled through a thick fog until slowly but surely the immense scale of the Dome operation came into view. At its center was a man-made sand island of 10 or 15 acres, which was used as a helicopter landing pad and on which had been stored piles of machinery, truck-sized anchors, rows and rows of 45-gallon drums and other supplies. Anchored offshore was a huge, floating dry dock, which was cradling two large tugs about 40 m in length. Nearby were two massive ships: one was a drill platform with a tall derrick and the other, apparently, some sort of repair or maintenance vessel. Several other small work boats, all of them quiet at this time of night, completed the tableau.

With all this to take in, it was a moment or two before we noticed the most bizarre feature of the scene before us: a life-sized coconut palm complete with climbing monkey, sculpted in steel and erected on the island by some whimsical welder.

When we landed, there was nobody around to greet us and we certainly didn't want to wake anyone so early in the morning. We hauled *Perception* up on the island and erected our tent near the palm tree. We must have made a startling sight for the crews of the ships when morning came: a Hobie cat, the quintessential tropical fun boat, parked on the sandy beach in the shade of their steel palm tree.

A rescue launch arrived to investigate us and we were invited onto one of the ships for breakfast. The *Wormlinger* was three stories high, a huge and very sophisticated floating ship-repair facility. Her vast bowels and deck held much of the machinery necessary to build a modern ship from scratch. We learned from Captain Peter Hughes that during the height of the Beaufort Sea oil exploration, this had been the busiest dry-dock operation in Canada.

We polished off an enormous lunch and, well sedated by the food, were soon enjoying the hospitality of the master of another vessel, John Cowan of the *Canmar Tugger*. He showed us around his ship where it lay in the floating dry dock moored alongside the repair ship. A gentle westerly wind had arrived that morning, and we had *Perception* tied up in the shelter of the *Wormlinger*.

John, Mike and I were poring over charts in the *Tugger*'s wheelhouse when I looked up at a snapping flag and noticed that the wind had suddenly backed around to the east and grown angry. *Perception* was now on the windward side of the ship, and in a rising sea, she would be in danger of being damaged!

We scrambled down a ladder and ran to the stern of the dry dock. My stomach lurched as I saw *Perception* being battered violently against the rusting hull that towered over her.

Our survival suits were three flights up on the ship's main deck. By the time we had raced up the ladders and down again, the squall had hit hard and the seas had built to the point where our boat's tall aluminum mast was swinging dangerously close to the ship and her steel anchor cables. I bounded down a ladder and onto *Perception* to try to fend her off, but the force of the waves was too great and I couldn't hold her clear. I was frantic.

Suddenly an exceptionally big wave struck us and *Perception*'s mast smashed hard against the barge. When she rolled back again, her leeward hull became pinned under one of the big tractor tires draped along the *Wormlinger*'s hull. Before I could comprehend what was happening, the two aluminum struts that supported the starboard wing on which we perched while sailing snapped like match sticks.

I screamed up to Mike, "We're being ripped apart! Get a boat!"

By now a dozen of the *Wormlinger*'s crew had appeared at the railing above us to watch helplessly as *Perception* was being pounded to pieces. Mike was down at the foot of the ship's ladder hanging on to our boat's bow line, while I managed to get a rope around one of the ship's anchor cables, trying to pull her off that way. But it was no use — the mast and hull kept banging against the barge. At one point, the mast was snagged under the railing on the barge's deck and bowed alarmingly before slipping free with a loud *twang*.

I was near despair when the tug *Arctic Sun* appeared

alongside like an angel of mercy and someone threw me a line. The tug quickly pulled *Perception* out of harm's way and we beached her, bruised and broken, on the island. We were just in time to retrieve our tent, which the squall had snatched up and sent pinwheeling across the island toward the sea, dumping its contents along the way.

It was at about this time that I ruefully recalled our conversation with John Bockstoce aboard *Belvedere*. We'd broken his cardinal rule and were now paying the price.

When we'd carefully examined *Perception*, our worst fears were realized. Not only was the wing broken, but our 9-m mast had been bent into a slight arc about two-thirds of the way up. It was only about 10 cm out of line at the top, but we knew that even this amount of flexing might seriously have weakened the thin-walled aluminum structure. Was it too weak for us to risk continuing our voyage? No one aboard *Wormlinger* was prepared to hazard an opinion. Aluminum sailboat masts were not within their area of expertise.

I telephoned my father on the ship-to-shore phone to let him know about the damage; he contacted Hobie experts to try to assess the seriousness of the situation, but they were of little help. Normally, they said, either a mast breaks or it doesn't break — they'd never before heard of one being bent. One thing was clear, though: the chances of getting a replacement mast shipped north to us before the season ended were next to nil. When Dad called back, we discussed the problem at length and I finally decided to cautiously carry on in hopes the spar would survive.

Mike and I accepted a kind offer from the *Wormlinger*'s master to repair the broken wing, and early the next morning we watched as a pair of cheerful welders went to work. While Ernie Thomas stood on the strut on a steel welding table, Wayne Anderson held it in position.

Ernie lowered his mask and lit his torch. A few minutes later he turned off the torch, lifted the mask and said to me, "There ya are pal. Better than fucking new!" I hoped he was right.

But the mast could not be straightened without weakening it further, and it was to be a constant source of worry.

The one bright spot in the whole disastrous episode at the Dome site was that we'd been able to repair our radio by replacing a faulty antenna.

At about noon we were ready to continue our voyage, patched up and fortified by another enormous breakfast. We circled *Wormlinger* with a wary eye on our mast and waved goodby to the crewmen lining the rail, before pointing *Perception* across McKinley Bay on a northwest breeze of about 10 km/h.

Chapter 3

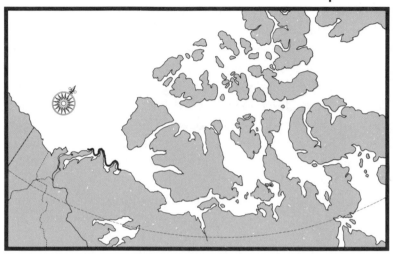

We were beginning to see a lot of ice now. Each of the floes and bergs looked different, in the way clouds do. One seemed to be a turtle floating on its back; another was shaped like a seal; still another looked like Snoopy, but closer up turned into a walrus. The ice reports we received in our morning radio schedules were anything but encouraging; for one thing, Amundsen Gulf, which we would soon have to traverse, was still completely impassable.

Two more days brought us to within sight of the Nicholson Island DEW Line radar station before we camped, sleeping out on the boat's trampoline after a magical all-night sail. We had watched the sun set just below the horizon at about 1 A.M., a shimmering orange globe that seemed to set the sky on fire as it tracked across the southern horizon before rising three hours later in a fresh blaze of glory.

The twenty-two stations of the DEW Line stretch right across the northern rim of the continent and were designed to give early warning of a sneak attack by Soviet strategic bombers. The development of such things as ICBMs, satellite surveillance, submarine-launched missiles and over-the-horizon radar made many of the stations obsolete as soon as they were built, but the Canadian government has continued to man them because they serve to enforce Canada's sovereignty over the sparsely populated north.

In the early hours of the morning of August 4, we saw our first caribou while camped on a bed of frosted dwarf willow and cotton grass near Cape Dalhousie. The sun had just dipped below the horizon and the animals looked magnificent silhouetted against the twilight sky. Mike held his arms up to imitate their antlers as he'd seen Inuit hunters do, but they would come no closer than a couple of hundred meters, and eventually they trotted away. Later we climbed the frozen dirt cliffs behind our camp to photograph a family of rough-legged hawks we'd spotted. While the mother soared overhead complaining loudly, we inched out on our bellies to get a look at their nest where it clung to the cliff face 30 m above the beach. Inside there were four downy chicks huddled together for warmth against the cold east wind, along with a dead ground squirrel, which the mother had been feeding them.

When we finally launched *Perception* that day, the wind had built to nearly 35 km/h and we really blasted along through meter-high seas up Liverpool Bay toward Cape Bathurst. At times, both of us were stretched out of the trapezes as we skimmed along flying one hull. It was sheer exhilaration.

In the near-calm that came just after sunset, we spotted an enormous barren ground grizzly bear foraging along the shoreline, his cinnamon coat making him difficult to see against the sand as we ghosted by. It was the first I'd ever seen, and I steered close in to shore for a good look. He, too, was curious and surprised us by wading out into the sea toward the boat. He must have weighed 360 kg and when he rose up, dripping, on his hind legs, he was more than 2 m tall. I steered back out to sea, praying that what little wind there was wouldn't die, but the bear apparently disliked what he'd seen of us and dropped back on all fours. He splashed ashore and lit out across the tundra with a speed that showed what formidable predators these animals can be. This was clearly no place to camp and so we sailed on into the twilight until the sun rose again at about 4:15 A.M. When we finally stopped, we'd covered 90 km, our best day so far.

Mike awoke feeling ill the next morning. The glands in his neck were swollen and rather than risk serious sickness, we decided we'd take the day off so that he could catch up on sleep. We'd been pushing ourselves too hard, sometimes sailing all night to go as far as possible when conditions were favorable, and fatigue was beginning to take its toll. Despite the superb cold-weather survival gear we wore, we were often cold and our feet and hands were numb much of the time. The only place it seemed possible to get warm was in our sleeping bags.

By August 6, as we sailed along the rim of Franklin Bay, we encountered relatively heavy ice. The water was about three-tenths ice-covered and sailing a straight course at speed through the bergs and floes that ranged in size from a car to a small house was a challenge — one that I thoroughly enjoyed. It was cold though — $-1°C$ — and the wind had a vicious nip. The highlight of the day for me came during a brief period when I was hiked out on the trapeze flying the windward hull. The sensation of hanging out over the water at top speed while the ice slipped by beneath me was thrilling, like skiing downhill through trees.

Mike still wasn't feeling well; he had a sore throat now and was having trouble keeping warm. Nevertheless he was anxious to drive the boat under these exciting conditions and I turned over the helm, not because I wanted to but because I felt I should.

Throughout much of the voyage there was to be an unresolved tension between us over the issue of who drove the boat. I didn't wish to be selfish, but I felt strongly that this was no place to be teaching someone to sail. The summer was extremely short, and the difference between sailing at peak performance and doing less well might mean many kilometers lost in a single day. It was also a fact that since my sailing skills were superior to Mike's, it was usually safer for both of us if I was at the tiller. Given the murderous antagonisms that blot the history of Arctic expeditions from Henry Hudson to Elisha Kent Kane, the strains that were to develop between Mike and me over this and other issues could only be considered trivial, though at the time they often seemed important enough for me to note them in my journal, where I would vent the day's accumulated spleen.

Selecting a partner for the expedition had been one of my most difficult chores. There were several qualifications I felt were important: skills in sailing, photography, camping, Arctic survival, navigation and compatibility with my personality. During the winter of 1986 I had developed a list of more than a dozen possible candidates, including people I knew from sailing, skiing and university. At the same time, I was trying to interest *National Geographic* in the story of our journey. Their major concern was the quality of the photography, and it was clear my chances of being published in the magazine would be minimal without help in that area. Good photographs were also important to fulfill my commitments to the expedition's many sponsors. As a result, skill as a photographer was pushed high on my shopping list, superseding skill in sailing.

In March 1986 I had had the opportunity to meet and talk with Bill Mason, one of Canada's most respected environmentalists and film makers. He suggested Mike Beedell as a possible candidate. This Ottawa photographer, he said, had spent many months over the past several years in remote areas of the Arctic, traveling alone and with others on wilderness journeys. He had recently published a fine photographic book called *Magnetic North*. He might have the skills *National Geographic* was looking for.

I contacted Mike, who was instantly enthusiastic about the idea of a boat trip through the Northwest Passage, though there was a distinct pause in our telephone conversation when I mentioned that the boat we'd be sailing was a Hobie cat.

"Are you crazy?" he asked.

"Absolutely," I replied.

"Well, I guess I'll have to come to Toronto to see how crazy you really are."

We met two weeks later in the city and later spent four days together camping and sailing a sister vessel of *Perception*'s in the springtime ice of Georgian Bay to see how we'd get along together. One day we hauled the boat over 15 km of ice to see whether we could do it. We could, but only just, and even though the ice was smooth compared to what we'd be encountering in the north, we managed to puncture a hull. It was then that we'd decided to construct a set of plastic runners.

There were certainly differences in our personalities, and Mike had little or no prior experience in sailing. But I felt his experience in Arctic survival, his ability as a photographer and his general good humor more than made up for whatever gaps there were in other areas. Beyond that, it seemed unlikely that I would find anyone else who shared with me the peculiar brand of insanity that makes one consider it fun to sail an open boat through ice-infested waters cold enough to kill a man in two minutes flat.

With the ice we were now encountering came curious harp seals, who would comically stick their heads out of the water to watch us fly by or, caught napping on an ice floe by our silent approach, would slide off into the water with a startled splash. They seemed fat and healthy and I envied them their warm coat of blubber. At night sitting outside the tent cooking dinner, we could frequently hear spouting beluga whales, though it was difficult to see them amid the ice.

That evening I listened to Bruce Springsteen on my Sony Walkman while I wrote in my journal. We'd just polished off a fine dinner of Scotch broth, freeze-dried lamb stew with mashed potatoes, hot chocolate and an apple. The page reads, in part:

"Unfortunately the splendid wind that set us in swift motion this morning died away soon after it began, and so we didn't go as far as I wanted to. We never do. But I must admit I'm loving every minute of our journey. . . . The wind is now calm, the sun has set. And a perfect day has been enjoyed. This is really living at its finest."

To our delight the morning brought a minor heat wave. It was warm enough after breakfast for us to remove our shirts for a few minutes to absorb a little sunshine. But our radio schedule brought disturbing news; the Canadian Coast Guard icebreaker *Martha Black* was holed up at Cape Parry, just 60 km ahead of us, waiting for ice conditions in Amundsen Gulf to improve before proceeding east.

It seemed to me from his tone of voice that the radio operator at Polar Shelf took a certain perverse glee in passing this bit of information on to us.

"Are you still heading on?" he asked.

"You bet!" I said. It suddenly seemed important to catch up with the icebreaker, if only to prove to the radio operator and all the other unbelievers we'd encountered that we could indeed navigate successfully in these waters with *Perception*. A Hobie cat in these parts no doubt provoked its share of double takes and snickers, and I knew the features that most people thought

made it hopelessly inadequate for the task were the very
features that in fact might make it possible for us to succeed
where more substantial vessels had so often failed. Namely,
Perception was fast; it could be paddled when there was a lack
of wind; it could be dragged across ice; and it could be quickly
manoeuvered off dangerous seas.

We were now into a period of light, fluky winds in which our
progress was frustratingly slow. In one hour-long period, the
wind shifted 180° around the compass and then back 100°.
Under such conditions, it was next to impossible to push
Perception along at her maximum potential. On one day in
which we spent fifteen hours on the water, we covered only
about 40 km, much of it paddling.

The combination of bad weather and slow progress began to
make me impatient. Small delays in getting underway in the
morning started to take on the proportions of major crises; I
couldn't understand why Mike wasn't more eager to get going.
I questioned his commitment to the expedition. Why was he
more interested in taking photographs than in making progress
toward our goal? Summer was so short, and we had so far to go.
Why wasn't he more concerned? I inwardly railed against the
injustice of the elements: why did eighty percent of the few
winds we did get have to be right on our nose?

But there were other moments, as we drifted, becalmed, when
Mike and I would laugh hysterically at the bits he'd read to me
from the book he'd brought with him, *Even Cowgirls Get the
Blues.* And in my more reflective moments, I was able to
appreciate the great beauty of our surroundings and feel
gratitude for the opportunity to be traveling in this wonderful
land. I told my journal:

*"The beauty and the calm make these periods magical. If a
far-off destination weren't our goal, I couldn't think of a finer
environment to gaze upon. Ice pans drifting past, curious seals*

*bobbing about and once in a while a mighty bowhead whale
entering the panorama. As evening descends the light becomes
magical, making our yellow boat glow."*

We had reached the region of the Smoking Hills, where
black, thirty-story cliffs facing the sea exude clouds of
blue-gray, sulphurous vapors. The smoke is the result of a rare
natural phenomenon; the cliffs contain huge quantities of
an unstable mineral called jarosite, which becomes red hot
on exposure to air. The burning jarosite ignites the black,
bituminous shale and the two burn slowly within the cliffs,
producing the vile-smelling smoke. They've been burning for
centuries, and the badly polluted tundra behind them has
provided scientists with a ready-made laboratory for studying
the long-term effects of man-made acid rain. We landed to
explore and take photographs. I found that when I thrust a
paddle into the shallow soil, the earth billowed smoke. Before
long, we'd both developed pounding headaches from the
poisonous fumes and we retreated quickly to the boat. The
effect was like climbing to the top of the Sudbury superstack
and stuffing your head in.

By August 9 we were down to fifteen days' supply of food in
our blue waterproof barrel, and Mike had fewer than twenty
rolls of unexposed film remaining. Cambridge Bay, where we
could reprovision, was almost certainly more than fifteen days'
distance, since our morning radio schedule placed the
icebreaker *Martha Black* just 8 km off Cape Parry, still waiting
for Amundsen Gulf to open. This was cutting things closer to
the bone than I'd planned, but there was no option since we
were moving so much more slowly than I'd hoped.

I pushed harder than ever to make progress despite the
uncooperative winds, at one point towing the boat along the
shoreline at the end of a 15-m length of rope. As long as the ice
floes kept out of the way, this was faster than paddling. With
the Smoking Mountains off to the north, we took turns trudging

along the beach with a line over our shoulder while the other steered the boat. When a slight breeze sprang up we followed the zephyr offshore, but a few minutes later we had to again resort to the paddles.

In the evening, we paddled wearily ashore to climb a ridge and scout our way ahead. We were halfway down Franklin Bay now and could just barely make out the opposite shoreline; we calculated it must be about 40 km distant. The ice cover on the bay seemed quite heavy, but it was difficult to know whether this was simply the foreshortening effect of our binoculars, piling everything up into a two-dimensional plane.

On our return to the boat, we saw a prowling grizzly nearby. Quickly we unloaded cameras, tripod and shotgun, but before Mike could point a lens at him he'd caught our scent and raced off into the hills at a remarkable clip. We slept that night with the loaded shotgun between us in the tent. Against the constant background noise of grinding and crashing ice floes, we imagined several times we could hear the footfall of a bear, but each time we checked outside there was nothing. In the morning, however, we discovered that our radio antenna had been knocked down.

I still hadn't decided whether to risk the long open water passage across the bay, or to play it safe and stick to the shoreline all the way. Conditions weren't encouraging when we departed that day. There was a heavy fog and the winds were light, though substantial enough to keep us moving. We tacked down the coastline for about an hour and a half until finally, I asked Mike, "What do you think? Is it too risky?"

"Let's give it a try," he said.

The bay at this point was about the width of the English Channel, and a crossing was not something to be taken lightly in so small a craft as ours, even in ideal conditions. The conditions we were facing were, in fact, something less than ideal: dense fog, three-tenths ice cover, highly variable winds and no guarantee that the opposite shore wouldn't be made inaccessible by ice.

What would we do if we were caught offshore in a storm and the way to land was blockaded by ice? In theory, the best plan would be to seek the shelter of a large floe and try to ride out the weather, but we had no idea if it would work in practice. (We were to find out in terrifying circumstances a year later.) The question became moot when halfway across the bay the ice thinned and then disappeared at about the same time as the wind did, leaving us to creep along, unprotected, at a desperately slow pace. A pair of playful bearded seals provided temporary diversion, and then we saw a loon and knew land could not be far away. Finally, five and a half hours after we'd set out, we reached the east shore of Franklin Bay, having won our first big gamble.

Once we had sighted land, Mike steered *Perception*, while I lay on the tramp reading *Arctic Breakthrough* aloud. My heroes were all here, among them Sir John Richardson, who'd named this bay, and Sir John Franklin, for whom he named it. Richardson, a brilliant polymath who'd begun his career as an Edinburgh-trained surgeon of great promise, had accompanied Franklin on both of the unlucky explorer's harrowing overland expeditions to the Arctic. He had seen hunger so extreme on these expeditions that men had boiled and eaten their boots to stay alive.

Richardson's final trip overland to the north at the age of sixty was undertaken as part of the first of the great searches for his former trail mate, who had vanished without a trace along with two Royal Navy ships and 129 officers and men while trying to find a northwest passage in 1845. Franklin's had been the best manned, best equipped expedition ever sent to the area; it had provisions enough to last for four years and the ships, *Erebus* and *Terror*, were specially reinforced against ice and outfitted with auxiliary steam engines. The expedition's inexplicable disappearance was as much a shock to the generation that spawned it as the sinking of the *Titanic* would be to their great-grandchildren.

The quest to rescue the Franklin expedition, and ultimately to learn how and where it had perished, became one of the great crusades of the Victorian era, and untold millions were spent by the British government, Franklin's indomitable wife, Lady Jane Franklin, and private philanthropists as expedition after expedition was sent into the north. It was during this decade of searching that much of the Canadian Arctic was explored and mapped for the first time.

Our landing site was Cracroft Bay, a place of enormous, wave-carved limestone archways first explored by Richardson in 1826. The sense of history here was palpable; however, I had other priorities at the moment. For water, I shaved ice from a floe that had grounded at the shoreline, and while Mike cooked dinner, I had a frigid but necessary sponge bath in the sea. It didn't take long: nothing inspires you to bathe quickly like sub-zero temperatures. But it had to be done. The wearing of several layers of clothing beneath a thick survival suit can cause problems of emergency access for the man of normal endowment. Both Mike and I got caught short more than once during the voyage. Such is the life of the adventurer.

Chapter 4

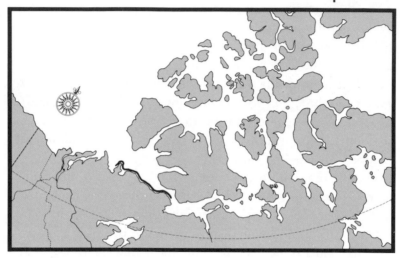

The elements continued to keep us from making much progress, even though new ice forecasts we'd received told us Amundsen Gulf was finally opening up. We left Cracroft Peninsula on August 11, 1986, in fog and a light breeze and before we'd gone very far the wind suddenly increased from almost nothing to more than 40 km/h. *Perception* was being overpowered and we ran for the lee shore with Mike trapezed out to keep us from flipping. The wind continued to build once we'd hauled the boat safely up on the beach, but the fog had vanished and in the bright sun the temperature rose to a balmy 9°C.

If we couldn't sail, I intended to keep busy. Stripping off my five layers of clothing, changing into a sweatshirt and pants, I hiked a few hundred meters inland to a shallow pond, clutching my dirty laundry and a bar of soap. Two pairs of Canada geese paddled unconcernedly on the water as I scrubbed away, using a half-submerged rock as a washboard. When I'd finished my clothing, I started on myself.

Mike was asleep in the sun when I arrived back at the boat with my heavy load of clean laundry. He awoke when he heard me approach, and seeing my clean hair, he grabbed the soap and a towel and trotted off to the lake. Later, while the clothes were drying in the wind, we stumbled on a Thule Eskimo site not far from the pond. The lichen-encrusted ruins of five stone and whalebone dwellings were just visible in the stunted grass. Mike thought they must have been 800 years old. The land would have changed little since then. It was not difficult to imagine the Inuit families going about their business, and it was as if their apparitions were with us as we stood and stared.

When the wind had moderated, we carried on sailing and late that night arrived off Cape Parry, where there was a DEW Line station. It had become important for Mike to get a fresh supply of film as quickly as possible, and the only way we could do that was through the Dew Line and their air supply system. We pulled ashore and walked a couple of kilometers to the airstrip to speak with the fellow who was holding down the night shift at the weather station. He wasn't much impressed with our story — it seemed we were the third boat to visit this week. *Vagabond II* had departed only yesterday and *Belvedere* was still in the harbor. We called up the radar station to ask if we could visit in the morning to use their phone to try to arrange for a film delivery, and the response was just as inhospitable: "Phone the station manager when he gets up." In pelting rain, we trudged back to *Perception* to set up camp.

In the morning, we sailed 4 km around to Police Point from Cape Parry, to get a little closer to the DEW Line station. We found the manager, a solidly built young man from Peterborough, Ontario, and I had a feeling he didn't think much of Mike and me. "Must be nice to have fuck all else to do," was his comment on our expedition. But he extended us a welcome in keeping with the northern tradition and we were given two rooms in which to stay the night. We spent much of the day on the telephone trying to arrange for a film drop at one of the stations down the line.

At dinner we stuffed ourselves with chicken, perogies, fresh milk, freshly baked buns, fresh vegetables, pecan pie and ice cream.

I played shuffleboard with Dick, the young station manager, and as the evening wore on he confided in me his reason for working on the DEW Line.

"I met this girl at the Becker's near where I live and we went out a few times. I just saw her a few times, you know, and then I hear she's pregnant and she tells me I'm the dad."

For a moment I imagined myself in his shoes and felt the hollow gut feeling he must have had.

"So I'm trying to lay low for a while," Dick concluded.

I thought to myself, "Cape Parry is a good place to lie low all right, you sonofabitch."

By midnight I'd developed a splitting headache. The bartender offered me two Tylenol and I headed off to my room. It was stifling, but I couldn't figure out how to turn the heat down. I pried the window wide open and left the door ajar to try to get some air circulating, but nothing helped. I lay on my bunk reading, wishing I was out in our tent. If it weren't for our shortage of film, I decided, I'd happily stay away from Dew Line stations for the rest of the journey.

At 9:30 the next morning we were out on the water in swells just under 2 m high, making good time in a brisk northeasterly wind. That same wind had piled ice several hundred meters deep all along the east shore of Darnley Bay, which meant that if we ran into trouble with the weather we'd have no real escape route. In these seas, the interface between the ice and the open water was a churning cauldron of mulch or brash ice and I wouldn't have given much for *Perception*'s chances there. Our safety margin was gone, but we had no choice but to press on, drenched in spray, my knuckles white on the tiller inside waterlogged gloves.

Before long, the swells had built to 3 m, and then the wind died. For a hellish thirty-five minutes we were left to pitch and roll in the steep seas while our stomachs protested urgently. Our kayak began charging into us from astern, banging away at the rudders and occasionally climbing right up on the trampoline and threatening to skewer either Mike or me. Then it broke free and we had to get out the paddles to reclaim it.

We could see that we were now being washed toward the heaving ice pack, and we paddled with increasing urgency to escape its deadly clutches. When the wind finally resumed, I steered for a small island about 2 km distant, where we planned to land briefly to try to walk off our seasickness and tighten *Perception*'s rigging. The starboard shrouds had been severely stressed in our accident at the Dome site, and we were afraid that if any slack were to develop, they might give way as the mast flexed. As for the mast itself, we had no real confidence it could withstand very much of this kind of weather.

Once safely ashore, we could see the full fury of the sea around us. Thundering breakers were sending curtains of spray 15 m into the air as they crashed into the limestone cliffs on the island's windward side. We stood there watching for a long time to be certain that we'd absorbed the lesson: these waters were dangerous and needed to be approached with respect and caution. A little farther down the shore we watched 1000-pound bergs being tossed like ice cubes onto the beach. Any one of them would have squashed *Perception* like a bug. As the sun set, it sent crimson flames spreading through the long ridge of cumulus cloud that marked the approaching weather front along the southern horizon. We spent the night.

The next day was Mike's twenty-ninth birthday, and we

passed it on our little island waiting out the storm. In the evening, while Mike was out exploring, I inflated some party balloons and dug out the bottle of wine we'd been given. When he returned, we relaxed and enjoyed a rare moment of reflection as Mike reminisced about his last seven birthdays, all of them spent above the Arctic Circle. I was beginning to get a feeling for how much he loved this frozen yet magical world.

We were across the 30-km mouth of Darnley Bay in less than three hours early in the following frosty morning, flying along through seas that were less than a meter high in a 20-km/h northeaster that cut like a knife. That meant we'd bypassed the village of Paulatuk at the foot of the bay and missed our chance to buy film for Mike, but I felt the saving in time was worth it. Mike was not so sure. I pointed out that there was still a good possibility the twenty rolls we'd ordered would turn up at one of the DEW Line stations ahead of us.

Rounding Pearce Point, we entered a beautifully protected harbor, which had a stunning key-holed limestone island that reminded us of Percé Rock. We camped near a derelict old RCMP post where Mike discovered the following inscription in ink on an inside wall:

BELVEDERE CREW

AUGUST 11, 1986

That put them just four days ahead of us!

We had moderate winds for much of the day, but they were mostly headwinds, which meant constant tacking. Mike steered for five hours, but I couldn't help thinking he spent too much time looking at the scenery and not enough watching the telltales on the mainsail to ensure that he was getting every last ounce of performance out of the boat. He just didn't seem to have a sailor's instinct and I told him as much, no doubt too bluntly. He replied a little sourly that he was an explorer, not a racer. I pondered that and tried to find the right words to explain why it was important to cover as much distance as possible when the wind was good — not just for the sake of the abstract goal of racking up the kilometers, but because we had so little time, and because so many people — our sponsors, in particular — were counting on us to do our level best. I could see how it would be difficult for him to feel the same pressure of responsibility as I did, since he hadn't been involved in planning the expedition, negotiations with sponsors, making commitments, accepting favors from friends. I wanted to say all of this.

What came out was: "Our sponsors didn't send us here to linger over the landscape. They want us to complete the passage!"

That wasn't the right thing to say to someone like Mike.

I tried to get some sleep on the trampoline but couldn't. I was too cold. I listened to *The Big Chill* tape on my Walkman for a while, but that soon palled. For the first time on the trip, I was bored with sailing. It was so frustrating beating into a light headwind kilometer after tedious kilometer.

We pulled *Perception* ashore when the sun dipped below the horizon at 11:00. Eleven! At Liverpool Bay it had set at 1 A.M. Summer was leaving us.

It was another full day before we got a favorable wind, and it was a day full of frustration. We filled the time paddling until we developed blisters. We went ashore, hiking and photographing caribou and seals. We tried catching Arctic char in the rivers we encountered, with no success. The kayak, increasingly becoming a dangerous nuisance, snapped the top off one of *Perception*'s rudders. We repaired it with three-minute epoxy and it broke again and we had to repair it once more. My back ached constantly and I didn't know why, unless I'd strained it pulling the boat ashore on the island during the storm. All I could do was pray for a strong westerly or southerly wind.

It was a west wind that eventually came upon us at

mid-afternoon on August 19. It began as a warm breeze, at first
not very strong; to take maximum advantage of it, we shifted
our bodies up to the front of the hulls. It began to rain heavily
and then a sudden, powerful gust hit us. I scrambled to the back
of my hull, but Mike was caught forward, trying desperately to
release the jib sheet. Before he could do that, *Perception*'s stern
lifted into the air and her bows dove beneath the surface. I
leaned back as far as I could but it wasn't far enough. Our whole
bow section was submerged now, and still the wind did not
release us. We were going to pitch-pole, end over end. Mike was
now chest deep in the frigid ocean and the water was well up the
trampoline. I clung to my high and dry perch, holding my
breath. Then, slowly, our forward motion stopped as the
buoyancy in *Perception*'s hulls asserted itself, and we popped
back to the surface like a cork.

The wind continued to stiffen, and while Mike roller-furled
the jib I steered for shore which, fortunately, was not far away.
We ran the boat right up onto the beach and the kayak washed
up behind us, smashing into the stern with frightening force,
luckily doing no damage. We looked at each other, unable to
speak.

When we'd recovered our faculties, we decided to give the
weather another try, this time with the main reefed right down
to the third reefing point. The wind was reading about 45 km/h,
a solid Force 6, and the waves were a manageable meter high. If
we stayed close to shore, I figured we would be safe enough.

But the waves quickly built and in the following seas, the
kayak was being driven into our stern. When it had capsized
twice — Mike righting it each time with enormous effort — we
decided it was time to land. By now the seas were running about
2 m high and as they crashed onto the gravel beach, they
unloaded tumbling chunks of ice ranging from football to
garage size. We couldn't slow down enough to proceed
carefully through the churning masses of ice being driven

ashore, so we blasted right through it onto the beach, hitting hard and leaping ashore to drag the boat out of harm's way as quickly as possible, while waves crashed over our heads. For the second time that day, we were lucky and escaped without a scratch.

The wind howled throughout the night, tearing at the thin fabric of our tent and threatening more than once to lift *Perception* bodily and toss her on her side. We laid the kayak across her bows hoping the extra weight would prevent the damage, and I awoke several times to check that she was okay. By morning the beach had been littered with ice of every conceivable size and shape and it took a great deal of effort to haul *Perception* through this mess and into the water. Finally she was afloat and as the sails bellied out and Mike and I dragged ourselves aboard, I looked back to see the kayak still on the beach! We jibed around to an ice-free stretch of shoreline and, while Mike held *Perception*, I dragged the blasted yak over 30 m of gravel, rock and ice.

We passed Clifton Point, entering the mouth of Dolphin and Union Strait (named for the two open boats in which Richardson explored this coast), and as we did so we heard an approaching aircraft. Mike fished out the aircraft radio and we called on the 212.5 MHz emergency channel. We could now see it was a DEW Line Fairchild and when the pilot responded, we switched to a general traffic channel to ask about ice conditions between us and Cambridge Bay. He told us that there was no shortage of ice ahead, but that it looked as though it might be possible to get through.

It was a break we badly needed; we'd come 1200 km in twenty-five days and still had about 580 km to go before reaching Cambridge Bay, our goal for this season. If our rate of travel remained unchanged, we had twelve days of sailing ahead of us, and only nine days' provisions.

Variable light winds plagued us for most of the day, when

there was any wind at all, and we paddled briefly before packing it in for the night near a promising-looking fishing stream. But we had no luck with our rod, either.

The next day began with Mike towing us down the beach in a dead calm. Then I broke the rudder where it had been repaired twice before, just as the wind put in an appearance. We'd reached a region of 85-m limestone cliffs, and Mike hopped from boulder to boulder at their base trying to catch the boat and climb aboard. We sailed on awkwardly, steering with one rudder, and rounded a point marking the end of the cliffs. As we did so, a mast appeared, tilted at a crazy angle. Then a beached hull came into view and we could see that she was a converted fishing boat. Her name was still visible — *Nechilik* — and she'd been aground there for a good twenty years judging by the rust on her plating. We took some time to explore her and in her forward cabin I found copies of the *Winnipeg Free Press* dated November 9, 1966, and January 3, 1967. An advertisement read, "Brand New Car, $1,499." Later we learned that she'd been an RCMP patrol boat and had been blown ashore in a gale.

We had another brief towing session with *Perception*, which ended in frustration because, with the broken rudder, I couldn't keep her clear of the shore. Mike walked back to the *Nechilik* to see if he could salvage a hose clamp or some other repair material while I started filing down a spare chain plate for reinforcing. I dug the foam out of the rudder core at the break, bent the chain plate and slipped it into the hollow before filling the broken rudder cap with epoxy and fitting it in place. Mike had returned with a hose clamp, which we cut to shape and screwed down over the break. Then the whole thing was covered with fiberglass tape and resin. It seemed to work.

We'd been concentrating so hard on our work that at first we didn't notice the sound. Then Mike said, "Can you hear it? Listen!"

It was the cry of a peregrine falcon that must have been nesting on the cliff behind us. The species has come close to extinction, thanks mainly to pesticides and poachers. We were traveling through one of its few remaining natural refuges, Mike told me. It was a poignant moment for both of us as we stood on the beach and listened to that haunting cry.

When we relaunched *Perception*, the fog had rolled in, though there was a good breeze, and we sailed on with visibility at about 100 m until, with a little help from our hand-held RDF (radio direction finder), we found the DEW Line station at Cape Young just at sunset.

When morning came, we hiked up to the station to ask the manager if Mike's film had appeared: it hadn't. Harry, the manager, was a crusty old gent who'd been in the Arctic for twenty-three years, strictly because the money was good. We couldn't get him much interested in our expedition and after we'd made small talk for a while, we left his office to return to the boat. As we passed the kitchen, our mouths watered at the delicious aromas. Ah, well!

We had reached the exit, when the cook poked his head around the corner and asked, "Don't you guys wanna stay for lunch?" We wouldn't turn down an offer, we said. He checked with Harry. "C'mon back. It's okay." We headed down the hall to the dining room, peeling off our jackets as we went, and dug in. Some of the technicians began to take an interest in our trip, and we answered their questions between mouthfuls, though our attention was occasionally diverted by the cheers and guffaws of half a dozen men who were watching a pornographic video. Morning on the DEW Line.

Our alacrity in accepting meal invitations at the DEW Line stations we visited had little to do with the quality of the food − though it was undeniably tasty − and even less to do with the surroundings. It was simply that Mike and I were always hungry. In planning the expedition, I had consulted several

nutritionists about provisions, and they recommended a daily
ration of a little under 0.7 kg of food or about 4000 calories each
per day. It was a carefully worked out compromise between our
need for sustenance and the need to keep the boat as light as
possible. Before we'd left for the Arctic, Cathy and I had
packaged each day's rations in individual waterproof bags. But
Mike and I burned up energy so quickly in our harsh
environment that we felt satisfied only immediately after
eating. The rest of the time, hunger gnawed at us.

That day we made good progress under sunny skies and a
moderate easterly until late afternoon when we rounded Cape
Hope and then Cape Bexley. Over our shoulders we were
watching a storm creeping up on us from the northwest, and in
the early evening our wind died and we were left adrift in an
eerie calm. Then the rain began, quickly turning to snow, and
cat's-paws began to ruffle the water. Within ten minutes, we
had 40-km/h winds, enough to force us to furl the jib as
we screamed along the shoreline. We were heading directly
downwind now and the waves were building rapidly. I knew we
were too close to shore, close enough to risk grounding on a
submerged boulder, which at that speed would have been
disastrous. Jibing to steer offshore seemed out of the question;
the wind was so strong now that the fiberglass battens in the
mainsail were being bent forward to the breaking point. If we
jibed, the boom would swing over to the other side of the mast
with such force that it could cause serious damage to the boat. A
jibe in these winds might also flip the boat over, at which point
Mike and I would be thrown into the sea and the mast would hit
bottom, in all likelihood snapping like a celery stalk.

My heart pounded in my ears as I fought to keep *Perception*
under control. I had been cold but now I was perspiring. We
both perched as far back on the hulls as we could, not daring to
stretch our aching muscles or to shift to a more comfortable

position for fear of upsetting the delicate balance of the rocketing boat.

I was sorely tempted to pull in to shore, but we were making such rapid progress — 30 km in the last hour under just one sail! — that I couldn't bring myself to throw in the towel. However, the seas continued to build and *Perception* began having real difficulty riding them. I was increasingly concerned about our damaged mast. We would slow briefly in the troughs and then the wind would catch our big mainsail and drive us up over the crest and bury our bows in the next wave, creating tremendous strains on the rigging. The trampoline was awash much of the time and Mike and I were whipped with icy spray.

Then we crested a large wave and were driven with extraordinary force right under the next. The whole boat — trampoline, both hulls, our big waterproof deck bag — was under a foot of water. It streamed around Mike and me, threatening to drag us off our precarious perches. For a moment we were a submarine, and then the forceful buoyancy of the hulls took over and we were sailing on the surface again.

Ahead of us through the snow, spray and darkness, we could see the land curving out to the left. If we were going to keep sailing, we would have to jibe to stay offshore. There were only a few seconds in which to make a decision. We scanned the shoreline and there, miraculously, was a sheltered bay. I steered into it and as we sped up to the beach, Mike and I jumped into the water to keep *Perception* from grounding with too much force. It felt wonderful to be standing on solid ground, and Mike gave me a congratulatory pat on the back.

We erected our tent with frozen, fumbling hands and crawled inside in the fading light to cook dinner. As luck would have it, the pump on the gas stove seized and we had to oil it and adjust the rubber sealer ring, not an easy job to do in the dark with numb fingers. Eventually, we got the thing working and made a freeze-dried dinner that, if not hot, was at least warm. It was midnight when we burrowed deep into our sleeping bags.

In the morning when we stuck our heads out the door of our snow-covered dome tent, we discovered we'd camped by an old Inuit site watched over by an *inukshuk*, a life-sized stone effigy of a human used in earlier times as a navigation marker, or sometimes to frighten game. It looked eerily human in its mantle of white.

Chapter 5

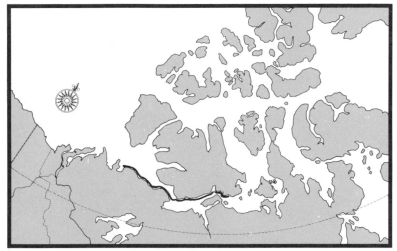

We were very close now to the jumping-off point from which we would cross Dolphin and Union Strait to Lady Franklin Point on Victoria Island. From there we would have less than 400 km of sailing to reach Cambridge Bay. Storm-bound in our tent all day, we pored over our charts and checked our supplies and equipment; we had food enough for just seven more days.

The northwest wind was still howling but the snow had let up when we set out the following morning. We'd reefed the main and still we screamed along, weaving through the ice at a terrific rate while throwing up great plumes of stinging spray. Now we had to contend with seas of a meter and higher and ice cover of five-tenths. Appearing dangerously close, the mauve and green sea bottom was clearly visible as we dipped into the troughs between waves. Sailing under these conditions was both exhilarating and exhausting. The level of concentration needed to keep the boat upright and to avoid a grounding or a shattering collision with wave-propelled ice was every bit as intense as in a downhill ski race, and the sensation became even more reminiscent of skiing when it started to snow again, this time with big, wet flakes that plastered themselves to *Perception*'s sail. We stopped only twice during the day; once when we'd run off the edge of our navigation chart and had to retrieve the next one, and the other when we went ashore briefly to jog up and down the beach to relieve some of the cold and stiffness that had set in. In the early evening, our hearts in our mouths, we rocketed through the jagged, foaming reefs protecting Cape Lambert as we steered for shore and the warmth and rest we needed so badly.

The storm increased in fury overnight and once again we found ourselves pinned on shore, this time within sight of our landfall at Lady Franklin Point across the strait. It was so tantalizingly near and yet, in this weather, so impossibly far away.

In the morning the wind had moderated somewhat, but sailing conditions were still marginal. We talked ourselves into launching *Perception* by agreeing that it would be for a test sail. If we found conditions too rough, we'd return to shore.

Cautiously, we set out. The boat seemed to be riding well, so we continued, rapidly approaching what looked like a solid band of ice before us. When we reached it, we found we could weave our way through without much difficulty. The ice had a calming effect on the seas and, briefly, we felt secure. The opposite shore was now clearly in sight from the boat's deck; we mustered our courage and steered toward it, into the open water of the strait.

Almost immediately, we regretted our decision. As we sailed out of the lee of a small island, the sea became a foaming cauldron where the steep waves met a strong riptide. Our trampoline and hulls were awash and spray leaped 2 m into the air. I wondered whether we should turn back, but when I looked over my shoulder the shore had all but disappeared. And then, suddenly, the sea became glass-smooth. We had sailed into a large area of very shallow water and though the wind blew with undiminished ferocity, there were no waves at all. We scarcely knew what to expect next in this *Alice in Wonderland* environment.

We reached Victoria Island surfing down the backs of 3-m seas, the spray flying over us in great sheets, and then we turned east again, following a compass bearing toward the Lady Franklin DEW Line post. By now Mike was desperately low on film and as we sailed past the station, he gave it many a wistful look, suggesting finally that we stop. I had no intention of stopping as long as the wind continued to blow and we were making such excellent progress toward our goal.

Later, as we boiled along down the shoreline, we spotted two musk oxen near the beach. They watched curiously as we sped by and then they turned to gallop away to higher ground, looking for all the world in their fluid grace like a couple of pack horses bearing big loads of hair. Once again Mike wanted to stop, this time to try for a photograph, but I had been waiting for this wind all month and intended to extract every last kilometer from it. Again, we kept sailing.

At 9:00, we were among the Richardson Islands, both of us very cold and very tired. When the wind began to die an hour later, I steered to Edinburgh Island and we dragged *Perception* ashore through the pounding surf. It had been a splendid day with lots of effort expended and lots of reward in return. We'd sailed for eleven hours and were now 160 km closer to Cambridge Bay: just 240 km to go.

In the morning, Mike pointed out a huge bull musk ox silhouetted against the horizon on the ridge behind our tent, his thick, ankle-length hair blowing in the gentle wind. As we climbed up toward him, he turned to face us with his massive skull and huge, downward-curving horns. We crept closer, keeping near the boulders for protection, and he began to snort and paw the ground like a bull in a *corrida*. This was the beginning of the mating season and this bull, who seemed to have misplaced his harem, was particularly frustrated. Mike took a few long shots and then I crawled closer, to within 5 m of the beast, so that Mike could get us both in the same frame. From this distance I could really appreciate the thickness of its long coat of hair, and how effective it must be at providing insulation. What a superbly adapted creature!

When we set out a little later, the DEW Line station at Byron Bay was our immediate destination — Mike still wanted to check for the film. The spectacular cliffs of Edinburgh Island were gilded by the morning sun as we slipped quietly by. We saw several more musk oxen, at one time stopping briefly while Mike splashed ashore to try, unsuccessfully, for a shot.

As the day wore on, the wind improved and we made excellent progress. The winds were perfect for sailing and we were humming along. I began to reexamine our motives for stopping at the station; we were within 150 km of Cambridge Bay and surely we didn't need twenty rolls of film for that distance.

I asked Mike if he felt we really needed to stop. He gave me a look of pure exasperation and said he did. Not wanting to provoke a serious confrontation, I agreed we would pull in, but only for long enough to inquire about the film. As soon as I'd made the decision I kicked myself for it, but it now seemed impossible to reverse my position. The result was that when we went ashore at 6 P.M., I was extremely angry with Mike for wanting to stop, furious with myself for agreeing to stop and frustrated in the extreme that we were wasting precious minutes in ideal sailing conditions.

I had hoped there would be a shore phone at the beach to save us the 6-km walk to the station to find out the film had not been delivered — as I was certain would be the case. But there was no phone and no response to a call on our aircraft radio either. As we set out hiking up the hill in search of the station, Mike commented that the wind appeared to be the kind that dies with the setting sun. That might be true, but the sun would not set for another three hours.

I strode on in angry silence, leaving Mike to follow behind at a more leisurely pace. I should have made a better decision for the expedition and ignored his desire to stop, I told myself. Why couldn't he understand how urgent it was to keep moving, keep moving, at all costs, before winter stopped us in our tracks?

Thirty minutes later the station was still not in sight. In my frustration I swore so loudly my throat hurt and my ears rang. In the end it took an hour to make the walk. Mike arrived mopping perspiration from his face twenty minutes later. The film was not there.

Borrowing the station's radiotelephone, I called my father to update him on our progress. He felt we should stop at Cambridge Bay and resume the voyage the following summer, rather than risk getting caught in the winter freeze-up. It was clear by now that completing the passage in a single year was out of the question and, given the conditions we'd faced, we both agreed that reaching Cambridge Bay would be a significant accomplishment. He reminded me that the month of September, just four days away, was a dangerous time for sailing in the Arctic, that storms can spring up in minutes and blow for two weeks or more. But I wanted to reserve the final decision for the last possible moment. If ice conditions were good, it might make sense to continue across Queen Maud Gulf to Gjoa Haven or even Spence Bay, to get clear of the ice that streams south in millions of tonnes down M'Clintock Channel each spring and chokes the approaches to King William Island.

We caught a ride back down to the boat with a couple of the station technicians and quickly donned our dry-suits. It was 9:00 when we pushed *Perception* back into the water — we had wasted three hours and 50 or 60 km of sailing. Easy sailing. I was furious and had to let Mike know how I felt. Trying hard to keep my voice under control I said, "I must tell you that this was the biggest waste of time of the entire trip. We should have kept going."

He looked up in surprise, apparently not comprehending our need to get to Cambridge Bay. He didn't seem to understand how important it was. He thought it was me who was pushing it — it became personal. I said he had to understand the expedition as a challenging goal and I was just trying to make sure we achieved it. He said he saw my point but preferred to stop more often; he said he usually traveled slowly, whimsically, in the Arctic. He felt we could take a morning here and an afternoon there to discover more about the environment and still make our destination. I replied that if he were in control of how we traveled, we would be hundreds of kilometres further back! He did not respond. Later he apologised, whether because he meant it or just to smooth things over, I had no way of knowing.

The wind remained steady and we made reasonable progress in the deepening twilight. The moon rose to light our way and then Venus made a brilliant appearance and the land became a dark silhouette off to our left.

Mike gallantly declared that he was keen to sail all night. At first it seemed a nice suggestion. Then I thought, "I know what this guy is trying to do to me. Last night he was complaining about sailing into dusk at 9:30. He even asked, 'Are we going to find a place to camp or sail until midnight?' Now, tonight, he wants to go all night. He's trying to cover his ass, look keen."

When the wind dropped at around 11:00, we put in to shore and quickly and silently set up camp. Mike put up the spare tent, sensing that a little space was needed. He was right. I was in my sleeping bag before midnight but could not sleep. I was livid at having allowed the DEW Line stop today. In missing those three hours of ideal conditions, we'd sacrificed the distance we'd covered in an entire average day — two days if we had poor winds. I could not calm myself and was awake much of the night, turning over the day's events in my mind again and again.

The temperature dropped to $-8°C$ during the night, cold enough to chill us inside our sleeping bags. When we emerged from our tents, there was heavy frost over all our exposed gear, and a solid layer of ice had formed along the shoreline. Winter was showing its hand, no doubt punishing us for our slow progress. My anger was strong, but internal.

I quickly began to pack, doing most of the work by myself while Mike busied himself at his usual pace. I had promised myself not to be held up by him again. I pulled on my dry-suit and then dragged *Perception* into the ice-crusted sea myself. I returned to shore to hook up the kayak and pulled *Perception* down toward the point. Mike got the picture and started to hurry.

The wind wasn't strong enough to propel us through the newly formed crust of shore ice, and so we paddled for half an hour, struggling to reach open water. When we did, we were overheated and worn out. We sailed across Byron Bay but compared to the previous day, our progress was so excruciatingly slow I felt like jumping ship. For thirteen hours we pressed on, fighting the fitful east wind, until exhaustion forced us ashore at twilight. We'd covered just 50 km.

Once again I was cold all night in my sleeping bag, and when morning came I was still exhausted. My hands and feet were numb. We ate dry granola while wandering a little inland where Mike found an above-ground Inuit grave. A chill gripped me as Mike peeked into the weathered, white wooden box. I couldn't bring myself to look over his shoulder. He told me it was the remains of an old lady who was clutching a cross. He snapped some photos to record this strange mixture of Christian and Inuit traditions, the cross and the exposed grave, and then we walked back to the boat and suited up for the day. The blustery east wind seemed to slice right through me.

As we pushed off, I was overwhelmed by fatigue and became quite dizzy. I pulled myself aboard and we set out. My only desire was to keep moving.

As we rounded the point on which we'd camped, we were exposed to the full force of the east wind. The sea was so rough we could not risk sailing directly across the mouth of Wellington Bay, and so we turned into it. I feared we might have to sail right around the coast of this deep inlet and was prepared to do that – anything to keep going.

Fortunately, the winds dropped and the sea became calmer and we edged out into open water. Mike steered while I sat with my back against the mast, trying to regain my strength.

The wind kicked up again once we were across the bay, forcing us ashore for two hours. We huddled in the lee of *Perception* and cooked a meal. I drank deeply from a nearby stream, hoping to get some fluid back into my dehydrated body.

At 6:30 we edged back out into the angry sea and, by tacking back and forth up the shoreline, made slow but steady progress. When exhaustion overtook us, we went ashore at an inlet called Starvation Cove, hitting a sharp rock in the process and ripping a 20-cm gash in the outer gellcoat of one of the hulls. We heated some soup and were asleep minutes after eating it.

The east wind was hammering at our tent when my alarm woke me at 7:00, and I reset it for 8:00. Still the wind was too strong. We called Tuk for our regular radio schedule, but got no response, so we dressed and carried our transmitter and antenna up the desolate, black outcropping behind our rocky campsite. Tuk was still not receiving us, but we finally reached Resolute and were able to relay our position and tell them all was well. Ravenously hungry as always, we broke into our last day's food supplies. Starvation Cove seemed an appropriate venue for our meal.

Seen from our vantage point above the beach, the sea looked anything but inviting. The strong east wind had blown it into a froth of white crests, though how high the seas were we could not tell from our height.

Under normal circumstances, I would have voted to wait for conditions to moderate. But these were not normal circumstances.

We donned our dry-suits and set out, moving close to the protected western shore of our little cove. Too close, in fact — within minutes our dagger board crashed into a rock and was badly ripped. We shoved it back down into its slot and kept going.

As we reached the point and were exposed to the full force of the wind and waves, we were horrified by the size of the 5 to 6 m roller-coaster swells.

Though it took a heavy toll on our nearly depleted reserves of fortitude, once we had mentally adjusted to the scale of the seas, we found we could ride them reasonably well. We sailed on, trying desperately to keep alert, and watched anxiously for any sign of a rigging failure. We punched out into the seas far enough to round the point and then tacked northeast into the long shallow bay. Somewhere ahead lay the settlement of Cambridge Bay.

Tack after tack, we crept up the bay bucking the powerful headwind and trying to avoid capsizing as we rode the steep swells. This was sailing at the outer limits of the capabilities of *Perception* and her crew, and neither Mike nor I could allow our attention to waver for an instant. He was handling the jib sheet, and I had the tiller in one hand and the main sheet in the other. My soaking fingers were numb, and to keep a grip on the rope I had to wrap it around my wrist. All along the steep, barren shoreline of the bay, crashing breakers made a landing impossible and so we carried on, though I was pushing my stamina and strength to a dangerous degree. I badly needed to relieve myself but could not safely move even to turn the tiller over to Mike. I fought off the inevitable for a few minutes and then felt a spreading warmth that left me as wet and uncomfortable as I'd been since I was a baby. On we sailed in the torrent, hour after hour.

It seemed like an eternity before we could see the 120-m high radio tower in Cambridge Bay. We swept in to a more protected basin where channel markers appeared and twice we thought we had rounded the last of them when another bobbed into view. Finally, our path was clear and we surged straight downwind at maximum speed into the heart of the village with its collection of Arctic bungalows, fuel tanks, storage sheds and administrative buildings.

It was 7:15 on the evening of August 29 when we reached our winter harbor and stumbled ashore on wooden limbs. I hugged Mike and we mechanically set about securing *Perception* for the night. Bill Lyle, the Territorial Co-op president, came down to the beach to greet us; he'd seen us sail in from the window of his house on the bay. At the little Co-op hotel I stepped into the men's shower still wearing my dry-suit, and as the steamy hot water beat down on me, I stripped off one layer of clothing after another until at last I was naked in the glorious heat.

Gale force winds were making our little hotel tremble the next morning, but Mike and I had to go out on the water again to satisfy the needs of a CBC film crew who'd been waiting for us and who had to fly out that afternoon to meet their deadline. The icebreaker *Martha Black* was in the harbor and they'd arranged to use its helicopter to film us sailing. The seas in the harbor bay were still extremely rough, but we were well fortified by the lavish dinner of Arctic char the women of the hotel had prepared for us the night before. I was not, however, prepared for the devastating effect of the chopper's prop wash, which very nearly tore our rigging apart as the big machine swept over us at mast height. Then we sped back to the town beach, easily outdistancing the big red and white icebreaker, only to wait two hours for the TV crew to prepare to film our "arrival."

We learned from the captain of the *Martha Black* that ice and weather conditions were rapidly deteriorating along our route ahead, and that John Bockstoce had abandoned his attempt at the passage for this year, taking to heart the advice he'd given us: "Never sail up here in September." Weighing all that information against our mast and rigging problems, I decided to interrupt our voyage where we were and return to continue next year.

Two more days were spent readying *Perception* for winter storage in a fishing warehouse in Cambridge Bay and sorting our equipment, and on September 1 I flew south for Toronto. Mike left for Ottawa two days later.

YEAR TWO — 1987

July 31 – September 6

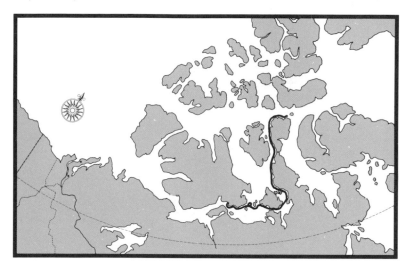

Chapter 6

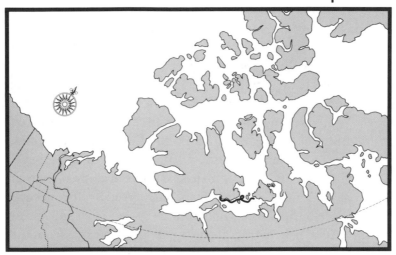

We returned to Cambridge Bay on July 27, 1987, with 280 kg of gear stuffed into half a dozen duffel bags. A new mast, wing and shrouds for our battered Hobie cat had arrived by air the day before. Mike was at the airport to meet me, looking fit and weather-toughened. While I'd been attending classes in business administration and going about the tedious job of drumming up sponsorship for this second, and I felt sure, final year of the Polar Passage expedition, he had been on an exciting Arctic journey. As part of a five-man expedition retracing a fabled nineteenth-century Inuit migration from Baffin Island north to Ellesmere Island and across Smith Sound to Greenland, Mike had traveled overland by dog team for 3000 km in the depths of winter, completing the journey late in June.

In considering that winter how best to proceed with my own expedition, I had decided to enlist the support of a championship Hobie cat sailor from the United States to make the "dash" from Cambridge Bay to Pond Inlet. The plan was for him to meet us in Gjoa Haven, where Mike and I should arrive about the time of year that open water is at its maximum. My own sailing skills had improved a great deal during the previous season, and I felt reasonably confident about tackling the notoriously dangerous waters of Franklin Strait, Peel Sound, Barrow Strait and Lancaster Sound – but not if I was going to have to do all the sailing. The twelve- to fourteen-hour days I'd put in driving the boat the previous summer had taken me to the limits of my endurance, and all the experts I'd spoken with during the winter had assured me I could expect sailing conditions to be even more arduous this year. To a man, they'd told me I should find an experienced sailor to accompany me on the final leg, and I couldn't help but agree. I felt I needed someone on the boat who would be able to share the load and at the same time help extract the ultimate performance from the cat.

Mike, by now deeply committed himself to the idea of sailing the passage with me, had only reluctantly agreed to continue documenting the voyage after Gjoa by meeting us at various predetermined points and spending a day or two photographing our progress. I knew he was not happy with this arrangement, but I felt I had to put the success of the expedition above his personal feelings.

At 8:15 on the morning of July 31, Mike and I hauled *Perception* down the beach at Cambridge Bay and raised her sails against a stiff northwest breeze. We no longer had the bothersome kayak in tow – on balance it had been more trouble than it was worth and I'd decided to leave it behind. It had given us an extra margin of safety, in theory at least, but it had also endangered us and the boat on many occasions by ramming into us from astern in following seas. It also took a long time to load and unload it once on shore. I'd spent many hours working out ways to lighten our load so that we could dispense with the kayak and found that by eliminating our spare tent, spare stove and fuel and several other back-up items, we could get along without it.

In the process, we had streamlined our equipment storage to minimize the time it would take to pack each morning. This was accomplished by designing two neoprene duffel bags with waterproof zippers. The waterproof bag we'd had the previous year had proved too large to carry when loaded. Cathy designed and constructed cordura and webbing outer bags to protect the neoprene and allow us to carry them more easily.

We also developed a better way to use the storage space within the hulls of the Hobie. There was lots of capacity there, but with the only access being two 20-cm diameter hatches in each hull, it was difficult to fit things in. Cathy designed nylon stuff sacks that would fit through the openings and stand upright along the bottom of the hulls. By making efficient use of the hulls and the two new duffel bags, we were also able to dispense with the big plastic barrel we'd carried on deck and in this way eliminated a lot of unnecessary resistance to both wind and breaking seas.

Our severe weight restrictions had not permitted us to increase the size of our daily food rations, but several other changes were made. We switched to a freeze-dried food that could be cooked right in its foil pouch by adding a little boiling water. That meant we'd save weight by cutting down on fuel for the little Coleman Peak stove and by not having to take along our big cooking pot. It also meant we wouldn't have to wash dishes in the freezing sea water as we'd had to during the first summer.

During the long winter, I'd also adapted a set of skis for *Perception* that I hoped would solve the problem of ice jamming up inside the plastic runners that we'd experienced during our training sessions. The skis were an old pair of Fischers I'd raced on in Europe, modified with fiberglass mouldings to fit into the dagger board openings and cup the banana-shaped hulls where they began their steep upward arc. We stored them under the two wings.

Finally, a big, brightly colored spinnaker was added to our sail inventory to help us maximize open water and light winds.

The harbor had been blown clear of ice, but as soon as we'd negotiated the navigation markers we were confronted by a solid line of white stretching from shore to shore. I aimed for a spot where the going looked relatively smooth, and we pulled the boat up onto the pack. It was just possible for the two of us to drag *Perception*'s 270 kg along, hopping from floe to floe, wading through the melt pools and crashing through the rotten ice in their depths, all the while hauling on the two wings. Before we'd gone very far, Mike suggested we try strapping on the plastic runners we'd carried with us all the previous season without using.

That was the ticket. We raised the mainsail for some extra push and began to make steady progress. The effort had us sweating profusely and before we'd gone far, we'd stripped off the tops of our dry-suits.

After nearly six hours of this, we had spanned the 10 km of ice and *Perception* splashed into open water. Up went the spinnaker and off we glided down a band of ice-free water along the coast of Victoria Island. The exhilaration of being underway again, the big maple leaf chute flying, was tremendous.

We sailed on far into the night, dodging floes and at one point hauling *Perception* over a narrow band of ice that was blocking our way. The effort caused a twinge of pain in my abdomen, but I soon forgot about it once we were underway again. We slipped quietly past a young ring seal asleep on a small piece of ice, so close that I nearly touched him with my outstretched hand before he awoke and leaped as if for his life into the sea. At 2:30 A.M. Mike suggested we get some sleep but there was no way I was going to waste a single minute in good sailing conditions on this or any other day this season. I wanted that precedent firmly established from the start. He eventually pulled out his waterproof bivouac sack and catnapped on the trampoline. But it wasn't long before the frigid sea spray forced him back onto the wing. At 4:30 the wind became too strong for safety and only then did I pull in to shore, after twenty hours at sea and more than 130 km sailed.

We were up again five hours later, groggily surveying our surroundings in Parker Bay. A weasel in summer brown entertained us with a hilarious series of flips, rolls and leaps on the tundra not far from our tent. We were roaring with laughter as we watched this tiny circus act by a performer who'd probably never again have a human audience.

There were spectacular pressure ridges erupting 10 m and more out of the ice that still blockaded part of the bay. But there was open water leading eastward, and the northwest breeze we'd enjoyed all the previous day had resumed.

I felt an urgent need to get underway as quickly as possible, but we'd both grown unfamiliar with the routine of decamping and packing the boat and it was more than four hours after we'd risen before we were underway again. I found this frustrating, and told Mike that it just wouldn't do, that this year on a normal morning when sailing conditions were good we needed to be on the water within an hour of waking up.

"Fine," he said. "We've got to make good time, no question. But we also have to sleep now and then. Miss too much sleep and you begin to make poor judgments, and up here that's fatal."

All I could do was put him on notice that I intended to complete the voyage in as short a time as possible, and that there would be other nights when we'd be sailing through till dawn if the wind was good. He accepted this, no doubt understanding as I did that we'd have to push ourselves to the limit to succeed.

We launched *Perception* in silence and found a lead opening in the direction of Jenny Lind Island. When it closed in front of us, we pulled the boat onto the ice and dragged her several hundred meters through melt pools and around pressure ridges to where open water resumed.

The wind had stiffened now, and the waves built steadily as we flew along toward another band of white across the horizon. As we approached it, I picked what looked like a promising lead and we sailed into it, only to reach a dead end. We turned around and sailed back out, and into a second channel through the ice. Another dead end. This time we stopped at the head of the lead and Mike climbed on my shoulders to look for openings in the pack. There was open water ahead but it was rapidly being filled in and we suddenly realized that the wind and current were conspiring to imprison us in the grinding, moaning ice. With a desperate effort, we dragged the boat across the drifting pans to where the water remained free, and we sailed down a fast-closing lead.

We were overjoyed to find that it opened into what seemed to be a huge expanse of open water. In moments, we had raised the spinnaker and I was once again enjoying the thrill of a high-speed slalom through the ice adrift on the current along our path. We hadn't gone far, though, when we once again found our way blocked by solid ice, and we turned north into a lead that soon closed around us, leaving us stranded.

We hauled *Perception* up onto a pan about 2 m thick, retrieved our shotgun from the waterproof deck bag and went in search of a pressure ridge or piece of rafted ice that would give us enough elevation to survey the ice around us. There was no open water visible anywhere, from horizon to dazzling white horizon.

There was nothing we could do but stay where we were and

hope the wind and current would break up the pack to set us free — and do it soon. We pitched our tent on the boat's trampoline and before retiring made sure all our gear was organized for an instant departure, should our ice floe break up or a lead appear in the pack.

As we marked time the next day, still imprisoned, we took some small satisfaction from the fact that the current had carried us about 10 km east during the previous twelve hours.

To keep ourselves occupied, we decided to mount one of Mike's cameras at the masthead with a remote shutter release, hoping to get some good pictures of *Perception* and her icy surroundings. While the boat was lying on her side with the mast at ice level, it occurred to us to rig a line to climb the mast so that we could survey the ice for ourselves. Mike tied a series of foot slings in a rope and attached it to the masthead. When we'd righted the boat, he cautiously ascended the mast, being the lighter of the two of us, while I photographed him. Then I too climbed the mast and took in the glorious view, though it depressed me to see ice in every direction. From this height we could see nearly 2 km in every direction.

Looking at the ice from the mast convinced us that we'd be in a better position to take advantage of any leads that might open if we hauled the boat to the north side of the huge pan on which we were camped. The hulls had frozen into the ice and it took a great effort to get her moving. In the course of that struggle the pain I'd had in my abdomen since the first day out became quite intense. I mentioned it to Mike and he said he thought it might be a hernia, a condition about which he seemed to have surprisingly extensive knowledge. Warming to the topic, he went on to tell me how hernias are treated by opening the abdomen and stitching together the rip in the abdominal wall that has allowed the intestine to slip through. The operation must be followed by a long convalescence, he assured me.

He was really getting into the subject now and regaled me with tales of how even the fittest of voyageurs had often died of strangulated hernias, which, he carefully explained, occur when the muscles in the abdominal wall are so strong they pinch the displaced loop of intestine, cutting off its blood flow. Gangrene results, and the victim dies a lingering, agonizing death.

I felt sick just thinking about it. Could it be possible? What would I do if it were true? That night I dreamed of us being frozen in the ice and then coming upon a huge stone mansion that looked haunted. Then, suddenly, I was in an airplane that was somehow clinging to the near-vertical side of a mountain, and we were preparing to take off.

We had one more day of enforced idleness and then late in the evening of August 3, I climbed a tall spire of ice and discovered that a lead toward Jenny Lind Island had opened in the pack about a kilometer away. The intervening ice was rafted and hummocked and would be difficult to negotiate, but we decided to give it a try. We'd been imprisoned in this icy hell now for forty-seven hours.

It took just an hour to haul *Perception* to open water on her ice runners, though several times in the process she crashed down off ridges and hummocks with such force we thought we'd broken her. But she survived, as did my worrisome abdomen, and we were once again afloat, sailing through heavy ice cover toward the island. When we reached shore, we were forced to walk the boat through a maze of boulders in thigh-deep water to get her to the beach. One of the feet in my dry-suit developed a leak and by the time we'd set up camp, my foot felt as though it were frozen solid. I slept that night with my feet wrapped in clothing.

In the morning, we set out up the barren hill to the Jenny Lind DEW Line station perched high on the tundra slopes, with its forest of antenna towers and big, white radar dome.

From the hill, the ice in Victoria Strait looked virtually

continuous. But in the afternoon a report from a DEW Line aircraft put the ice cover between Jenny Lind and the Royal Geographic Society Islands at about six-tenths. And when we climbed part way up the radio tower, we could indeed see some open water to the northeast.

Shortly before 8 P.M. we pushed *Perception* down the beach and into the water, sailing cautiously through the boulder-strewn shallows and then navigating the near-shore ice. Eventually we found a lead to an open area of water and began to thoroughly enjoy ourselves, sailing along under a fiery orange sky with dumpling clouds. Since it was impossible to steer a compass course this close to the magnetic pole, we were navigating with Mike keeping the RDF pointed at a radio beacon on Gladman Point. For two hours we made steady progress toward the not-yet-visible islands.

Then a solid barrier of ice developed, curving up from the south. This did not greatly concern me, because there was still some open water farther north. We entered a broad lead that looked so promising we raised the spinnaker, but within twenty minutes we'd been brought to a standstill by encroaching ice. We hauled up on a floc and Mike ascended the mast, only to report that our situation looked bleak. There was ice everywhere.

We had no desire to repeat the frustrations of being ice-bound and scrambled to get *Perception* into the water before the pack slammed our back door. It had already closed part way, and we had to drag the boat over 100 m of ice to refloat her in the lead we'd just come up. We retraced our route searching for another opening in the direction we wanted to go, but there was none. In the end we were forced all the way back to Jenny Lind, cold, discouraged and exhausted after eleven hours of fruitless effort. We were greeted by dozens of snow geese and their noisy broods of goslings waddling across the tundra. Later, one of the DEW Line technicians trekked down from the station to watch us setting up camp. He looked *Perception* over with the air of a skeptical buyer in a used car lot.

"Wouldn't catch me out there in that," he offered with a Scottish lilt.

We fell asleep praying for a storm heavy enough to break up the pack.

During the next three days we developed a routine. We'd sleep in our tent, climb the hill to the station in the late morning first to check ice conditions and then to see what treats the cook had to offer. We'd read a magazine or watch a video or make small talk with the men before making a final check and returning despondently to our tent. One evening Mike and I were treated to the unappetizing sight of an obese technician watching a porn video called "Fat Chicks." But once the initial jolt of surprise had worn off we found ourselves rather disgusted. This was not my idea of high adventure in the Arctic, nor Mike's, but the plain fact was there was nowhere else for us to go.

I occupied myself for a long afternoon laying out our situation on paper and weighing the possibilities. Under "Options," I wrote:

1. Go straight for King William Island 160 km away, pulling the boat on its runners and sailing where possible.
2. Pull the boat south in search of an open lead to the east in the first-year ice of Queen Maud Gulf.
3. Wait here on Jenny Lind for conditions to improve.

Then I wrote, "Reasons to Stay," and under that I listed:

1. Safer for the crew.
2. Safer for boat and equipment.

3. Less tiring for the team, which still has a tough summer ahead.
4. Weather and ice reports do not look promising.
5. Quicker access to possible openings to King William Island.
6. Ice forecasters think conditions will improve if we wait.
7. Two unknowns: a) how much abuse our boat can take in an extended haul; b) whether we'd be able to ride out a storm if caught out on the ice.

Next I wrote "Reasons to Leave."

1. Summer is quickly disappearing.
2. The ice may not improve.
3. We may miss the ice window on the west side of King William Island, beyond Gjoa Haven.

It was a desperate time, and the fact that I was resorting to making lists confirmed it. It seemed an insoluble conundrum.

On August 8, encouraged by another aircraft report of six-tenths ice cover between us and the Royal Geographical Society Islands — this time from a friendly navigator aboard a Canadian Forces Hercules — we set off once again in a 35-km wind out of the northwest, under a heavily overcast sky and fog. It was 2°C.

The Geographical Islands lay to the northeast and we checked our bearings carefully with our RDF. But most of the leads we encountered took us more north than east and the farther we went in the fog-bound maze that had ensnared us, the less sure we were of our dead-reckoning position. Each time we ran into a band of ice, we hauled the boat over it and continued on our way, expecting at any time to see the islands taking shape before us. After eleven hours of this, convinced by now that we were lost, I called a halt and we pulled *Perception* up onto a sheet of thin first-year ice with what little strength we had left. Not only were we ice-bound once again, but we had no clear idea where we were. The horizon was empty in all directions.

We slept in our Gore-Tex bivy sacks on the trampoline with the mainsail raised, ready for an instant departure. When we awoke the following day, visibility was a little improved, and we thought we could see the faint loom of land away on the northeast horizon. In every other direction there was nothing but ice.

We made a determined effort to find our way out of the labyrinth, alternately sailing up promising leads and dragging the boat over ice to more open water. But there was not much hope left in us and when the wind piped up to 50 km/h and it began to rain and the fog rolled in, our situation was little different than it had been the previous night, except that we had lost sight of land altogether.

The wind that night was so violent that as we lay exhausted in our sleeping bags under the protective dome of our tent, we could feel the trampoline lift alarmingly beneath us. Several times the entire 400-kg mass of *Perception* and her burden of supplies, equipment and crew was shifted on the ice. This was no longer my idea of a good time.

Chapter 7

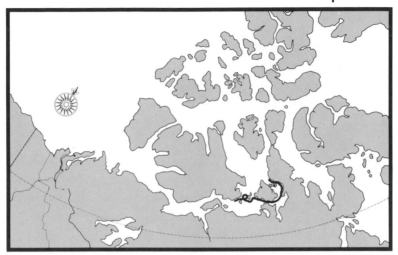

By noon the following day conditions had improved somewhat: the strong winds had gone, and with them the rain; the fog had cleared to the extent that we had about 1-km visibility. I took several very careful RDF bearings on the beacon at Gladman Point and off we headed into a broad lead that had opened along our course to the northeast. We were able to maintain this bearing for about fifteen minutes before the ice forced us to grope our way northwest and then west and south in a series of ever-narrowing channels.

Slowly the day degenerated into more backbreaking, frustrating, bone-chilling labor as the fog thickened and we crept from lead to lead, hauling *Perception* over ice pans and around bergs and hummocks in a jumble of first-year and multi-year ice. Our course was so erratic it was once again impossible to keep track of our position, especially since we hadn't been sure where we were when we'd set out.

Each time a lead opened before us we would agonize over

whether we should follow it, for even though it might take us in the opposite direction to the one we wanted to travel, there was always the possibility that it could, somewhere along its length, connect with an open-water route leading southwest. On the other hand, once committed to following a lead, there was seldom any chance to retrace our path, for the openings invariably pinched together behind us as the ice floes continued their kaleidoscopic motion. I found it enormously frustrating that so many of our decisions seemed to be wrong, until it occurred to me that perhaps there were no "correct" options available to us.

Aircraft observations we'd heard at the Jenny Lind DEW Line station had put the ice cover we were experiencing at six-tenths, though it seemed much heavier to us. The same reports warned that conditions ahead of us on our route to Gjoa Haven were worse, with ice cover of nine-tenths. I began to wonder whether we were going to have to wait until next year for the ice to clear enough for us to make it through this section.

Our efforts, persistent to the point of exhaustion, seemed so utterly futile that I became depressed and angry and began cursing our luck, cursing the ice, cursing the fog. Disagreements between Mike and me over which leads to follow became sharper; his choices were always wrong, but then so were mine. Mike, though, managed to maintain a more optimistic outlook through all of this and I guess my attitude finally got to him.

At one point he exploded with, "Well, I suppose I might as well be down on everything, too."

I thought, "Yeah, you're right. Don't let factors you can't control discourage you."

We stopped for dinner in the dense fog and freezing drizzle and in the lee of the boat I primed the stove. My hands were so wet and numb I could not make any of our three lighters work and finally used a match to get the fire going. While waiting for the water to boil, I munched on the raw freeze-dried food right out of the package. It tasted quite good, rather like potato chips.

Before we'd finished eating, the heavens really opened up. We moved *Perception* to a large floe of thick, multi-year ice where there were several good observation peaks and set about the business of making ourselves a home for the night. The boat was positioned with her bows into the wind to present the smallest possible profile and the mainsail was lowered and then tightly furled. We removed the boom from the mast and cleared the trampoline of its scramble of ropes, and then pulled the tent from its storage place beneath the forward waterproof hatch in the starboard hull. The aluminum poles were assembled and the nylon fabric of the tent clipped on. Once the dome had taken shape, we slipped the gray rain fly over top and secured it to make the structure watertight. While I lashed the rear of the tent to the front of the trampoline, Mike assembled the tent's vestibule where we stored the gear we wanted to keep dry and lashed down his end.

Next we threw our Thermorest insulating mattresses inside along with our sleeping bags and spare clothing, candle lantern, Walkman, food, stove, notebooks and other gear we thought we'd need during the night. Finally we peeled off our dry-suits, left them in the vestibule and crawled into the tent, safe and dry, we hoped, for another night.

When morning came on the third day on the ice, the fog had cleared and, for the first time in forty-eight hours, we sighted land.

It was not where we expected it to be.

Thinking we must, surely, by now be quite close to the Royal Geographical Islands, we peered into the east but could see nothing. Mike found his 500-mm telephoto lens, and we looked through that. Still nothing. Then he swept the horizon 180°, and directly behind us, he could see brown cliffs on the horizon.

"What the hell is that?" he asked.

For a few moments we were utterly disoriented, and then we realized that the land we were seeing was Victoria Island. The ice had forced us far off course into an 80-km long, semi-circular arc to the northwest that left us no closer to the Royal Geographical Islands than we'd been when we left Jenny Lind — we were just a lot farther north. A short time later, we confirmed our position by locating Jenny Lind Island off to the southeast.

We were numb with frustration, and it was some minutes before we could even begin to think of what to do next.

Our best option seemed to be to drag the boat across the ice toward Victoria Island, where we could expect there to be open water along the shore. Once in it, we might be able to find an opening to the east. Given the tortured ice-scape that faced us, this would be an arduous task, so we decided to scout the shore ice on foot before moving the boat. For the first time since we'd left Cambridge Bay, the sun came out — like an omen.

While Mike loaded a camera and started out, I ducked back into the tent where I found a small nylon stuff sack I'd packed in Toronto in anticipation of a time when our morale would need a boost. In it was a red top, red pants, red tuque, black belt and a white beard. I quickly slipped them on over my dry-suit and presto — Santa Claus! When Mike looked around to see me following him dressed as St. Nick, he seemed a little stunned. As soon as he recovered, he made a series of photos of me along our walk.

We trekked gingerly across floes of single- and multi-year ice for nearly two hours, until we came to the edge of a broad bay of open water. By then the sun had vanished again and the fog had begun to roll in, so we turned quickly to retrace our steps.

To our dismay, the pack had begun to open up and what had

started out as a simple walk to Victoria Island and back became a desperate scramble to reach *Perception* before we were stranded. Running as fast as the treacherous, uneven surface would allow, we bounded from floe to floe, my Santa suit flapping around me. It must have been a ludicrous sight. Twice when our route was blocked by open water, we commandeered a small piece of ice and paddled it across to where the pack resumed. Mike was leading and doing it with great skill, testing each floe and then nimbly leaping from one to another. Often the pieces he jumped on submerged under his weight. I followed him, holding my breath, knowing that I weighed 14 kg more and that I had the RDF and our aircraft radio in my day pack, neither of which was waterproof and neither of which we could safely do without.

We were about three-quarters of the way back when we heard an aircraft and I called it on our radio. It was a Northwest Territories DC-3 running cargo to Gjoa Haven. The pilot circled overhead so we could talk. He told us that open water lay not too far ahead of us, wished us luck and headed off to Gjoa, the destination we'd been struggling vainly to reach since we'd left Jenny Lind Island three days earlier, and which he would reach in a little less than an hour.

I managed to get back to *Perception* before Mike and set about boiling water for dinner, encouraged by the leads we could see opening everywhere around us. Maybe we'd break out of this ice prison after all.

Mike yelled at me from a nearby ice pan: he couldn't get to the boat and needed the Sea Seat, our one-man survival platform, to cross a widening lead I'd been able to leap only a few minutes earlier. I tossed it to him on the end of a line and he inflated it and paddled across. With his shaggy beard he looked for all the world like Neptune on his throne. Neptune and Santa Claus: here we were all dressed up and no place to go.

By the time we'd finished eating at 10 P.M., a lead had opened

in the direction of Jenny Lind and we debated whether to
pursue it, or give in to the demands of our weary bodies and get
some much-needed sleep. Several times I climbed the ice knoll
that was our observation post and stared at the water. It seemed
to extend about 500 m toward the island, not really far enough
to make it worth our while to explore. Once I decided to give it a
try and then promptly changed my mind. I climbed the knoll
yet again and something said, "Go." Mike was keen to try and
so we began packing our gear.

We were immersed in this chore when a huge bearded seal
startled us by sticking its head out of the water about 3 m away
from us. He must have weighed about 350 kg, and his curiosity
was insatiable. Over and over again he raised his body half out
of the water to peer at us with his intelligent, coal-black
eyes.

We set sail as the moon rose, blood red and spooky, the first
time we'd seen it on this expedition. A little after midnight, we
broke out into open water north of Jenny Lind Island and
steered east once again toward the Royal Geographical Islands
with Mike drawing a bead on the Gladman radio beacon with
the hand-held RDF. For six hours we sailed on, dodging
floating ice we could barely make out in the dim twilight,
shivering in the intense night-time cold, until we were stopped
by an impenetrable barrier of granite-like multi-year ice. It was
5 A.M. when we pulled *Perception* up onto the pack and pitched
our tent with the liquid fire of a sunrise seeping across the
sky.

Two more days of ice hauling and groping our way under sail
through the labyrinth of leads in fog and rain brought us at long
last to one of the most westerly islands in the Royal
Geographical chain, and after six nights out on the ice pack we
were able to camp safe and secure on solid ground. We were too
worn out to feel much elation. On the sandy shore there was a
group of beached, neon-pink jellyfish, still alive and pulsing.

Our Dodge Caravan at the Arctic Circle. The journey across Canada spanned 7,000 kilometers just to get to the starting line.
PHOTOGRAPHY BY JEFF MACINNIS / M.I.

The smoking hills of Franklin Bay stretch for nearly 80 kilometers. This devil's landscape emits deadly sulphur dioxide fumes.
PHOTOGRAPHY BY MIKE BEEDELL

Trapezed out to counter-balance the force of the wind, while navigating through ice-infested waters. PHOTOGRAPHY BY MIKE BEEDELL

A yearling polar bear cub seeks reassurance from a worried mother who has suddenly become aware of us.
PHOTOGRAPHY BY MIKE BEEDELL

Mike studies a set of huge polar bear tracks. The bear they belong to did almost an entire circle around us while we pushed Perception along.
PHOTOGRAPHY BY JEFF MACINNIS / M.I.

Santa Claus in the Northwest Passage. We learned that humor is critical in such an extreme environment.
PHOTOGRAPHY BY MIKE BEEDELL

In the glow of midnight Perception ghosts beneath 600-meter limestone cliffs. PHOTOGRAPHY BY MIKE BEEDELL

Our alternate source of propulsion—paddles. We must have paddled Perception more than 80 kilometers in total over our journey.
PHOTOGRAPHY BY MIKE BEEDELL

Kissing solid ground. Relieved to still be alive after a 16-hour ordeal that saw hurricane-force winds and 5-meter waves.
PHOTOGRAPHY BY MIKE BEEDELL

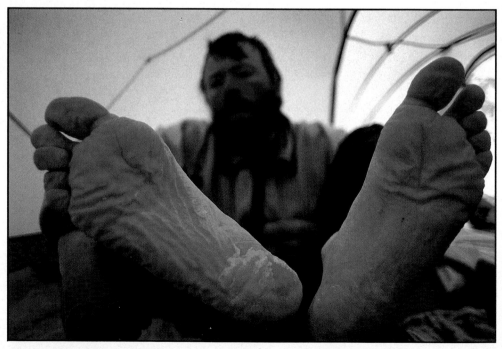

Mike's feet were badly frozen and wrinkled by immersion foot. Similar to frostbite, immersion foot is a result of exposure to cold, wet conditions.
PHOTOGRAPHY BY JEFF MACINNIS / M.I.

Ascending the 9-meter mast, Mike scans for open leads. PHOTOGRAPHY BY JEFF MACINNIS / M.I.

By the light of the moon we sailed through the night, but still couldn't quite reach land.
PHOTOGRAPHY BY MIKE BEEDELL

A moment of calm off the Tuktoyaktuk Peninsula.
PHOTOGRAPHY BY MIKE BEEDELL

A haunting reminder of past tragedies in the harsh Arctic. This is most likely a skull from an early explorer. The hole on the side is probably the result of a cannibalism bludgeoning.   PHOTOGRAPHY BY MIKE BEEDELL

Through the entire journey we were forced to haul the 450-kilogram Perception across some 50 kilometers in total. Here we are struggling off the Royal Geographical Society Islands.   PHOTOGRAPHY BY MIKE BEEDELL

Cape Anne: High winds and a windchill of -35°C forced us to build a snow-wall to protect the tent. Two days later we were forced to stop . Winter had arrived.
PHOTOGRAPHY BY JEFF MACINNIS / M.I.

Ice Camp. When forced to camp on the ice we would erect our Sierra design tent on the trampoline of Perception in case the ice broke apart while we slept. Not the safest feeling.   PHOTOGRAPHY BY MIKE BEEDELL

Mike photographs a mature Beluga whale beached at low tide in the Delta of Cunningham Inlet. PHOTOGRAPHY BY JEFF MACINNIS / M.I.

Jeff flying over large pieces of ice in Franklin Bay. PHOTOGRAPHY BY MIKE BEEDELL

They looked repulsive on the land, but in the water they moved with fascinating ease and agility, their thousands of cilia effortlessly propelling them as they worked and scoured the bottom. That night I had a horrible dream about deaths in my family and I awoke chilled through, frightened, hoping none of it was true.

August 12 was Mike's birthday, his second on this expedition. I slipped a "Happy Birthday" banner into the big waterproof map case stitched onto our mainsail before we set off. He seemed quite surprised and happy when he noticed it.

As we toiled on, winding our cold, wet, circuitous way westward, I began thinking of the ice as a metaphor for life's tribulations. The white barriers we faced often seemed impenetrable from a distance, but when we got close and began to probe there was almost always a way through. The route might wind and even take us backward for a time, but if we kept our eye on the target, it could be reached. Fortunately, life wasn't always this cold and wet. I found some solace in this notion at a time when it was increasingly difficult for me not to succumb to frustration.

In the afternoon we pulled ashore on a small island feeling weak from hunger and dehydration, even though we'd had our normal lunch. We wolfed down some salami and cheese and drank some slightly brackish water we'd collected from a melt pool. Our need for food was insatiable, and when we didn't get enough, it would affect us both mentally and physically. I was continually amazed at the speed and potency of food's effect on us.

Pulling, pushing, cursing, we inched *Perception* across a 70-m wide sand bar to avoid an 8-km ice haul around a point of land. When we'd recovered from that effort, we walked her through a kilometer of very shallow water to a lead that opened to the west, getting our feet soaked in the process. I had promised

Mike we'd stop at a reasonable hour and have a special dinner and a little rum to celebrate his birthday properly. But at 8 P.M., as we were considering where to set up camp, we noticed a narrow lead opening into the distance in the direction of our course. With open water ahead of us, we simply couldn't stop and so with a little more salami and cheese under our belts we carried on as the fog descended. We began to sing, "We all live in a yellow Hobie cat . . . ." and for a while I felt somehow like a detached observer. A vision crystallized in my mind of the two of us stumbling upon the lost Franklin ships, still throbbing with life, the cabins below deck lit with oil lamps. We would be offered rum and food by men as youthful and optimistic and determined as we were and be shown the library of 2000 volumes, including Dickens's newly released *Great Expectations*. At that moment, I felt the ice had forged a genuine bond between us and these doomed men.

The fog cleared at about 11 P.M. and we found ourselves close to another small island. Exhausted and numbed by the cold once again, but feeling a sense of genuine accomplishment for a change, we pulled the boat ashore and set up camp on a grassy knoll. Then we went about celebrating Mike's birthday as best we could. I turned on my Walkman with its tiny speaker and Mike poured us each a glass of the cognac he'd hidden away in his belongings. While the spaghetti heated in its pouch, we babbled cheerfully and with real enthusiasm about our prospects. After dinner we savored Snickers bars and finally drifted off to sleep at 1 A.M., feeling no pain.

The next morning I had all the classic symptoms of a hangover as I switched on our HF radio for our schedule. My mind cleared instantly, though, with the electrifying news relayed from Toronto that my father was at that moment on a French research ship holding position over the wreck of the *Titanic*, preparing to make a dive. What a trip that would be, down 4 km to see that fantastic ghost ship! My thoughts went with him.

For me, this was to be the worst day of our long ordeal in the ice pack jamming Queen Maud Gulf. We got underway late, after a long hike to scout for leads had left us confused and divided over which of several options to take. Predictably, we'd no sooner begun to sail down a narrow lead than the fog descended. After feeling our way through the gloom for some time, we found ourselves right back where we'd started, at the campsite. We tried a different tack, dragging *Perception* down the shoreline over ice and through boulder-strewn shallows, and after two hours, we found enough open water to take us to another island.

As we climbed the height of land, I became filled with an ineffable sense that our luck was about to change, and I broke into a run.

But when we reached the summit, all we could see was an unbroken jumble of ice, veined by a few narrow, meandering leads, none of which seemed especially promising. More of the same! My optimism plummeted. In the gathering darkness, we sailed into a lead until it closed down on us and we were stuck once again. I stepped onto a pan, slipped and hit my leg hard. I sat there, utterly dejected.

"This ice is winning," I said to Mike. "It's getting us."

I felt I had been beaten, mentally and physically. I had poured every resource I possessed into this venture, my heart and soul, and now the elements were defeating us. It seemed so unfair.

We maneuvered the boat to a tiny sand islet and camped there for the night. In my tortured dreams, no one I knew liked me.

I was in somewhat better humor when I awoke the next morning, able, at least, to muster the will to pack up and carry on. This is not to say I was enthusiastic, but then it's not easy to be cheerful — even when things are going well — when your day must begin by pulling on a pair of cold, wet socks.

Once again we set out following narrow leads as they opened and closed, weaving a path in the general direction of the most northerly of the Royal Geographical Islands, a tiny dot even on our large-scale chart.

The wind was high, as were the waves where there was open water; visibility was poor and the rain fell steadily. When we finally reached the island, I waded ashore and trudged up the hill to once more scout the ice between us and King William Island.

I could not believe my eyes. Open water! Miles of it! And all that was separating us from it was about 400 m of jumbled shore ice on the far side of the island. Mike joined me and we danced with excitement there on the barren hilltop.

It took us two hours to drag *Perception* across that 400 m of ice. Our pathway, if that's the word for it, was made up of a nightmarish conglomeration of pieces of ice — all sizes, shapes and ages, some rising out of the water as much as 3 m, all of it shifting, creaking and grinding away in the current, threatening to crush our legs if we took a false step. At times the boat's bows would be over our heads as we hauled it along on its runners, hoping it could withstand the stress and strain it was undergoing. The routine was simple: "One, two, three, heave!", and we'd move a meter or two forward. We'd check our position, change direction if necessary, and do it again. "One, two, three, heave!"

One of these efforts ended in a scream of agony from Mike, as a hull rode up onto his foot. We quickly pushed *Perception* back far enough to release him and a careful examination fortunately showed no sign of permanent damage, though the bruising kept Mike hobbling for some time afterward.

By such small increments we gradually escaped from the

shore pack and into open water; two hours later we'd reached the bleak, utterly featureless mud flats of King William Island. Gjoa Haven, here we come!

The wind continued fair and we steered south down the island's western shore, across Terror Bay, until in the narrows of Simpson Strait we once more encountered ice and, unable to find our way through in the midnight gloom, pulled *Perception* ashore on the sandy, kelp-strewn beach of an islet called Etna. We wrapped our numbed and swollen feet in spare clothing and slid shivering into our sleeping bags after sixteen hours of exhausting effort.

We had reached a place that was peopled like no other corner of the Arctic — by the ghosts of the great Victorian explorers. Not far north of here was the spot where Franklin's ships *Erebus* and *Terror* were immobilized by ice for two years, and where, abandoned, they finally foundered. Had he made it just 150 km farther south, Franklin would have completed the discovery of the Northwest Passage by linking up with the coastline Thomas Simpson had explored from the west in an open-boat voyage, six years earlier.

King William Island itself was at one time littered with relics of Franklin's imprisonment, including the bones of some of his men. It was at Victory Point on the island's northern coast that Leopold McClintock's search party in 1859 discovered the stone cairn containing the only written record of what had befallen the expedition. On a printed form supplied to ships of discovery, and normally released in bottles to establish the drift of currents, the following words had been written:

28 of May 1847 H.M. ships "Erebus" and "Terror" wintered in the ice in lat. 70° 05′ N; long. 98° 23′ W. Having wintered in 1846-7 (sic. This should have read 1845-6) *at Beechey Island, in lat. 74° 43′ 28″ N., long. 91° 39′ 15″ W., after having ascended Wellington Channel to lat. 77°, and returned to the west side of Cornwallis Island.*

Sir John Franklin commanding the expedition.

All well.

Party consisting of 2 officers and 6 men left the ships on Monday 24th May, 1847.

A message of hope and promise. But around the margins of this note was scrawled another, more ominous message in a different hand:

April 25, 1848 - H.M. ships "Terror" and "Erebus" were deserted on the 22nd April, 5 leagues N.N.W. of this, having been beset since 12th September, 1846. The officers and crews consisting of 105 souls, under the command of Captain F.R.M. Crozier, landed here. Sir John Franklin died on the 11th June, 1847; and the total loss by deaths in the expedition has been to date 9 officers and 15 men.

F.R.M. Crozier   James Fitzjames

Captain and Senior Officer   Captain H.M.S. Erebus

and start tomorrow, 26th, for Back's Fish River.

With perhaps three months' salt meat and biscuit remaining to them, they had set themselves the impossible task of reaching the nearest Hudson's Bay Company post, following the Back River to Great Slave Lake 1600 km to the south.

Around the cairn were found vast quantities of ships' stores, everything from silver plate to mounds of woolen clothing to books from the ship's library, evidence of men lightening their load in preparation for a long journey.

Very close to where we were camped, at Cape Crozier, McClintock's party had discovered another grim relic. It was a boat that had been specially constructed for the trip down the Back River, lightly planked and powered by paddles rather than oars, and it was resting on a sled that had been built to carry it. In it were the skeletons of two men.

McClintock estimated the combined weight of the boat and sled, exclusive of the boat's contents, to be 1400 pounds or 620 kg, nearly two and a half times the weight of *Perception* fully laden. He listed the contents in this way.

"Amongst an amazing quantity of clothing there were seven or eight pairs of boots of various kinds — cloth winter boots, sea boots, heavy ankle boots, and strong shoes. I noted that there were silk handkerchiefs — black, white and figures — towels, soap, sponge, tooth-brush, and hair combs. Besides these articles we found twine, nails, saws, files, bristles, wax-ends, sailmakers' palms, powder, bullets, shot, cartridges, wads, leather cartridge case, knives — clasp and dinner ones — needle and thread cases, slow-match, several bayonet-scabbards cut down into knife-sheaths, two rolls of sheet-lead and, in short, a quantity of articles of one description and another truly astonishing in variety, and such as, for the most part, modern sledge-travellers in these regions would consider a mere accumulation of dead weight, and very likely to break down the strength of the sledge-crews. The only provisions we could find were tea and chocolate. Of the former very little remained, but there were nearly 40 pounds of the latter. In the after part of the boat we discovered eleven large spoons, eleven forks, and four teaspoons, all of silver. Of these twenty-six pieces of plate, eight bore Sir John Franklin's crest, the remainder had the crests or initials of nine different officers."

After my own recent experiences on the ice with *Perception*, the thought of these starving, scurvy-weakened, half-frozen men struggling to drag such enormous loads of largely useless equipment across the floes brought tears to my eyes.

Twenty years after McClintock's discoveries, Lt. Schwatka of the U.S. Cavalry made an overland trek to King William Island, where he found more bones and relics and learned from the Back River Inuit that thirty-five white men had died on the mainland a few kilometers to the south and east of our campsite, near Point Richardson on the Adelaide Peninsula.

The bodies found by the Inuit had been surrounded by many papers, but it wasn't until 1923 that Knud Rasmussen became the first white man to examine the site. He of course found no papers, but he did find a quantity of human bones, which he buried. The bones and skulls bore graphic evidence of cannibalism, many of them having been cut through by saws. In 1931 another group of bones was found on an island in eastern Simpson Strait, a stone's throw from where we had pitched our tent.

There is evidence based on Inuit folk histories that a number of officers and men of the Franklin Expedition survived in this region for several years, clinging to the hope of rescue. But the many rescue parties that did come concentrated their efforts for the first crucial years almost exclusively on the waters far to the north of here, around Barrow Strait and Wellington Channel, north of Peel Sound. One reason for this seems to have been the belief, widely held at the time, in a balmy, ice-free Arctic sea at the top of the world where we now place the Queen Elizabeth Islands – the thought was that Franklin must have discovered this sea.

There was another reason for focusing the search to the north, and that was the conviction within the British Navy that Peel Sound was perpetually blocked by ice and therefore could not have provided a route south for *Erebus* and *Terror*. Ship after ship had forced its way to its entrance, only to find it choked with ice.

But Franklin did sail down Peel Sound, and I intended to sail up it.

Chapter 8

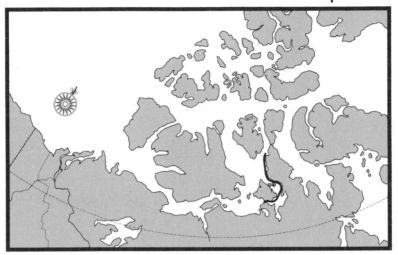

Two more days of sailing leads and dragging *Perception* over the ice brought us at long last to Gjoa Haven. They were not uneventful days. For part of the way we walked *Perception* in our ice-worn, leaking boots through shallows between the shore and the solid pack of last year's ice in Rasmussen Basin, until our legs were numb and lifeless from the knees down. When we'd finally come upon relatively open water, we'd nosed the boat into the sandy beach, jib furled but mainsail flying, so that we could do some jogging and jumping to try to bring some sensation back to our feet. This was a clumsy procedure, rather like trying to walk when both legs have gone to sleep. Mike jogged off in one direction and I in the other. When I'd gone about 40 m inland, I turned to see *Perception* drifting, stern first, out to sea with all our supplies and equipment on board. I screamed a warning to Mike, who was closer to her, but he couldn't hear me for the wind. I ran, stumbling, back to the beach and into the water, where I fell flat on my face. By now the boat was about 15 m offshore and her sail had caught the wind. I struggled to my feet and charged ahead through the water, finally lunging to get a handhold on her starboard bow in chest-deep water, my heart pounding in my ears.

Not long after that, Mike crashed through some rotten ice while we were hauling the boat and, clinging to the port wing for safety, very nearly dislocated his shoulder. We looked and felt like veterans of the Crimean War.

During these days we were able for the first time to use my old downhill skis on the boat. We were on the flattest stretch of ice we'd seen and with the skis, hauling *Perception* was about as difficult as walking a small dog. She glided over the ice, even with just one of us pulling. But when we encountered hummocks and rafting, the skis proved useless because the tips would catch on the slightest ridge or crevice.

Gjoa Haven was where Amundsen had been forced to winter for two seasons aboard his converted fishing boat, the *Gjoa*, during his conquest of the passage in 1904-6. He called it "the finest little harbor in the world," and sailing into her narrow entrance with its protecting hills, I had to agree. Today's Gjoa Haven is a village of 600 people, mainly Inuit, complete with airstrip, administrative buildings, hotel and an unusually colored collection of Arctic bungalows on stilts above the permafrost.

As we tacked back and forth into the harbor, we could see the red and white hull of *Vagabond II* still in her winter cradle on the shore and I felt a little tingle of excitement at the thought that we'd finally caught up with her. A crowd of about fifty people had come down to the shore to meet us. Mike shouted a greeting and they cheered. It was a magnificent moment.

Two crewmen from *Vagabond* were among the crowd, and in the absence of their captain, who was to fly in for the summer navigation season in two days, they invited us to dinner and offered us bunks for the night in the warmth of their cabin.

Conspicuously absent from the group on the beach was my American sailing friend who was to meet us in Gjoa. He showed up aboard *Vagabond* halfway through dinner, and immediately I sensed something was wrong. Then I learned he was booked on a flight south the next day. This was an enormous shock to me, but I tried to keep my feelings in check and to say as little as possible until I had come to grips in my mind with the problem. We walked back to the hotel where I took a much needed shower and then we talked, but the best I could do was to extract a promise that he wouldn't leave until we'd had time to analyze the situation further. I went to sleep in my bunk aboard *Vagabond* thinking this couldn't really be happening, that I'd wake up in the morning and find it had all been a misunderstanding and that I'd still have an experienced sailor with me for the sprint north.

It was not to be. It was obvious that the spirit had somehow gone out of him; that in the week he'd spent here waiting for us to arrive and listening to the locals talk about weather and the ice conditions, he'd become convinced that the voyage was impossible. I did my best to persuade him that we could indeed travel in these waters, and that his contribution was important to the expedition's success. But it was to no avail. My arguments didn't convince him and he left two days later.

Fortunately Mike was there to jump into the breach and this he did eagerly and with good grace, agreeing to complete the voyage. He was sensitive enough to keep to himself the thoughts to which he was entitled about my American hotshot and how he'd taken one look at the conditions he'd be facing and had flown back to the States. I was beginning to fully appreciate just how much of an asset Mike's fortitude and Arctic experience were to the whole enterprise.

We topped up *Perception*'s hulls with a thirty-day supply of food from the cache we'd had waiting here and traded our books and cassette tapes for fresh reading and listening material. We also did what we could to solve the serious problem of the leaking feet in our dry-suits. Gertie Brown, the wife of the school superintendent, had been recommended to us as the town's top seamstress and she kindly sewed tube-like nylon covers for our leaking boots. We coated them liberally with silicone sealant and hoped they would keep our feet dry. Jackie Radley, a bubbly young woman from Manitoba who was the town's recreation director, gave us the run of her house during the day when she was at work, so that we could go through our equipment in comfort.

In Gjoa we heard for the first time about David Cowper, a circumnavigating sailor who was trying to complete the passage from east to west. It was thought he'd run into trouble and was trapped in ice somewhere around Creswell Bay, 400 km due north of us.

On the evening of August 22, with *Perception* fine-tuned and in top shape, we sailed out of Gjoa harbor into Rae Strait, spinnaker flying, the bows slicing through water that was almost ice-free. I wondered if Mike would be up to the sailing challenges ahead. I also wondered if I would.

When we came ashore for the night about three hours later, a thin skin of ice had formed in a 30-m band along the shoreline and we tore through this in a shower of tinkling shards as we ran right up onto the sandy beach near Mathewson Point. We slept under the stars in our bivy sacks so that we'd be able to get an early start in the morning.

For three more days, we worked our way around the corner of King William Island, across Rae Strait to the mainland and north across Spence Bay to the Boothia Peninsula. The winds were very light and we did a good deal of paddling, a dreary chore made bearable by the fascinating landscape of rocks, underwater greenery and jellyfish and other creatures that passed beneath our hulls. One evening we were passed by two Inuit in an aluminum motorboat. They'd just killed a small

30-kg seal and the animal's head hung out the back of the boat, its nose dripping blood. A little later we passed a slick of scummy brown oil, a disgusting sight, and on the small island where we camped for the night, we were treated to the sight of garbage, including a crushed Coke tin.

On the evening of August 25, the wind finally returned, blowing hard from the east and giving us hope that it might clear the ice in Larsen Sound and Franklin Strait ahead of us. When we'd set up camp at our landing place near Oscar Bay, Mike went exploring while I boiled water for dinner. He returned in a few minutes with a piece of paper that he read to me:

20 May 1952

Patrol of RCM Police, left Spence Bay 18 May last for Cape Adelaide or Ross 1831 Magnetic Site searching for sign of Franklin Expedition of 1845. No dog food. Weather stormy since departure. Resting dogs today. Native Barney Equalla acting as guide. Csts Sergent & Hering. (Signed) 14698 J.M. Hering Cst.

Before returning it to the cairn where he'd found it, Mike added our names, the date and a greeting for the next explorers to find the previously unopened vial.

It was a vivid reminder of the days in which RCMP patrols had been the principal means by which Canada had maintained her sovereignty over the Arctic. Just two or three days' sail north of us at Pasley Bay was the winter haven of the *St. Roch*, the little RCMP vessel captained by Sergeant Henry Larsen that in the early years of World War II had planted the Canadian flag firmly at either end of the Northwest Passage by sailing it both ways. While the ship had lain beset by ice during the winter of 1940-41, her crew had busied themselves with the oddly bureaucratic chore of taking a census among the Inuit of the region. This involved giving each native a small metal identification tag to wear around his or her neck, bearing a number and letter code. In a ledger book, the census takers had carefully marked down the name of each Inuit beside his or her code.

The wind had built so much overnight that it kept us pinned to land for most of the day. I was quietly reading a book in the lee of a huge boulder when Mike startled me by thrusting a human skull at me. On an exploratory hike, he'd found old fire pits containing charred bone fragments and the skull, which was of some considerable age and in which a hole had been smashed on one side. This could have been evidence of cannibalism and the skull may well have been of archaeological interest but, like all sailors in the embrace of the elements, we were superstitious, and we had no intention of taking the relic on board *Perception.*

When we did get out on the water, it began to snow for the first time on this leg of the journey. It brought forcefully to mind the worrisome fact that *St. Roch* had been frozen in for the winter at Pasley Bay on September 6 — just ten days away — and we still had 2100 km to go to reach the eastern end of the passage.

A light aircraft flew over and we contacted it by radio; it was John Bockstoce of *Belvedere* out on an ice reconnaissance in a chartered plane. His vessel was still in Cambridge Bay. John confirmed that David Cowper was locked tight in Creswell Bay and unlikely to get out this season, and he said *Vagabond II* was now in Spence Bay, well to the south of us.

John also gave us an ice report, and conditions looked encouraging, though we both knew that a simple shift in wind direction could change the picture overnight. Cape Alexander immediately to the north was clear, he said, and it was relatively clear farther north around the Tasmania Islands. Bellot Strait was blocked and there was a lot of multi-year ice jamming the east side of Somerset Island. He strongly recommended that we continue north up Peel Sound rather than try for the shortcut through Bellot Strait and up Prince Regent Inlet; the Peel Sound route was the one he planned to attempt himself in *Belvedere*. Though there was a potential saving of more than 100 km using the Bellot Strait route as *St. Roch* had, the odds were that we'd be hopelessly blockaded by ice if we tried it. All of this information was invaluable to us, of course, and we were greatly indebted to John for his generosity in passing it on.

Fog forced us ashore that night and we set up camp in real darkness. It wasn't until several minutes after we'd landed that we noticed that the boat, the sails, rigging, everything was covered in a layer of ice. And there was more snow the next day as we wove our way through three-tenths ice cover up to and across Pasley Bay, making excellent time in the strong southeast wind. The low, rocky hills off to our right were obscured by fog much of the time.

During a wild, reefed-down ride up the coast and through the rocky channel east of the Tasmania Islands, we counted five polar bears in an hour and a half and when we found we could no longer cope with the fury of the wind, we had to set up camp just around the corner from them. In scouting for a place to pitch our tent, we stumbled on a seal carcass that had been stripped to the bone by ravenous bears. Our night was an uneasy one, haunted by dreams of marauding animals. In the morning we awoke to find 5 cm of snow covering the land, but we were intact.

There was a fair, fresh wind, but the tide was slack when my alarm woke me at 4 A.M. Much of the ice impeding our passage to open water in the sound was no longer afloat, the pans now resting on the bottom and tilted at crazy angles. Still feeling the effects of yesterday's exertions in near gale-force winds, I crawled back into the tent and returned to the warmth of my sleeping bag. I said to Mike, "Let's wait a couple of hours for the tide to float the ice." He didn't argue.

But at six, the ice was even worse. I kicked myself now for

having delayed our departure, losing two critical hours of good sailing conditions. We gnawed on a frozen breakfast of granola and dried fruit as we hurriedly broke camp. Soon the boat was ready to be hauled down to the shoreline and across the ice that had jammed our small bay. The next hour was punishing; the boat's hulls were battered unmercifully as we manhandled her across the jagged ice, and Mike and I crashed through into sub-zero sea water with every few steps. Though our dry-suits protected us from the worst of the cold, it was nonetheless an exhausting ordeal. The morning was half gone by the time we cleared the shore pack and were able to launch *Perception* into relatively open water. We set the main and jib and steered north, searching for a way through the ice into the open water we expected to find in Peel Sound.

But there was no way through. It seemed that while we had slept, the winds had completely barred the door. I reluctantly turned *Perception* around and sailed despondently the short distance back to the northernmost of the Tasmania Islands, where we scrambled up the gravel slopes of a high ridge to scout our way ahead. Through the binoculars, we could see that the ice formed only a narrow band across Franklin Strait, and that beyond it was open water with only three-tenths to four-tenths ice cover.

Half an hour later, we were hauling *Perception* onto the ice, confident now of reaching the open water beyond while the favorable wind held. Ahead of us lay the adventure of our lives.

Chapter 9

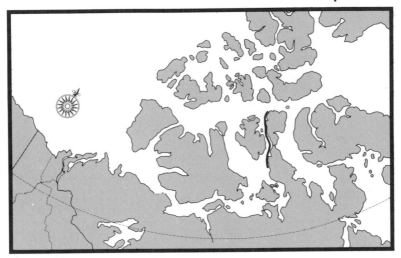

Mike was first to notice it as we paused to catch our breath – a
flock of glaucous gulls attacking a bloody seal carcass on the ice
off to the left of us. As we jumped from pan to pan to get to the
scene, it became obvious this was a very recent polar bear kill.
The blood-stained tracks told us a sow had been feeding her
cub, and though we had seen or heard nothing, it seemed clear
that we had frightened the animals off just as we had sailed up.
Intestines trailed off into the water as though each had taken a
last mouthful before fleeing. There was blood everywhere.
Mike knelt before the steaming carcass for a moment and then
reached into the body cavity. From the seal's womb he
extracted a perfectly formed pup and placed it, dead, on the
snow. I shuddered and checked over my shoulder.

We returned to our boat with a renewed respect for the
stealth and power of the polar bear, and I rehearsed in my mind
the strategy we'd worked out for dealing with bear attacks.
There's an old trapper's tale that says the best way to defend

yourself against a polar or grizzly bear attack is to shoot your buddy and run like hell. Our own preparations had been somewhat more sophisticated. Our first line of defence was a small marine air horn that made a very loud noise — the idea was that the animal would be frightened off by the blast. Next, we had hand-held bear flares, which are fired in the same way as a conventional marine flare, but go off with a much louder bang. Finally we had our nickel-plated, 12-gauge shotgun. It held seven cartridges and we'd loaded it in carefully ranked order of deterrence, from scary to fatal. First in the chamber was a rubber bullet, the kind sometimes used in riot control. Next came bird shot, which would do serious damage only at very close range. And ultimately there were five rifled slugs that packed enough punch at close range to stop a bear in its tracks, or so we hoped.

Before long we had traversed the ice and were afloat once again, running before a southwest wind that was steadily building. I steered a winding path among the floes as the pack opened and closed around us. We made rapid progress all the way to Cape Hobson and then across Wrottesley Bay, sticking as close to the shoreline of the Boothia Peninsula as the ice would permit. The waves were getting bigger and steeper, though still quite easy to handle, and we sailed on not wanting to waste a moment in these near-ideal conditions.

At 4 P.M. we once again found our way blocked by what appeared to be an impenetrable ice barrier. We stopped to scout ahead on foot and after a few minutes' searching, we found a lead opening to the north across a few hundred meters of relatively smooth ice, a short distance from where we'd left the boat. We sailed *Perception* around and with the following wind we were able to run her right up onto the ice. In a few minutes we were afloat again in the widening lead, making excellent progress for another two hours, until the wind started to drop. Up went the spinnaker and we surged ahead again, flying downwind into Peel Sound, the mainsheet straining and the rudders humming.

By nightfall the wind had freshened to the point where the boat was becoming unmanageable under full sail, and after fourteen hours of almost continuous sailing, I was reaching extreme exhaustion. It was time to quit, but the problem was finding a place to camp on shore, since the entire eastern coastline of Peel Sound was blockaded by a deep fringe of ice. We decided to go ashore instead on the rocky outcropping of Barth Island, which our chart told us was only a few kilometers ahead in the gloom. It was midnight before we pitched our tent on a reasonably level, rock-strewn patch of the barren shoreline.

My alarm woke us at 6 A.M. and we arose stiff and still weary, but anxious to once again take advantage of the excellent sailing conditions. In two hours we were on the water, raising the spinnaker to make the most of the freshening southwest breeze. The morning treated us to some of the most exciting sailing we'd had, surfing down the seas on a broad reach, hiked out on the windward wing, dodging the ice pans that littered our course.

At noon, we stopped briefly on a large pan to have a hurried lunch but by the time we were under sail once again, conditions had taken a dramatic turn for the worse. An angry-looking sky had rolled over our heads like a shroud and the wind was now whipping a light, crystalline snow in our faces. The seas had built to the point where it took the utmost concentration to avoid capsizing. It was starting to get ugly.

As she crested a wave and began to rocket down into the trough, a sudden gust overpowered *Perception*, driving her bows into the sea right up to the front cross-member; Mike and I had to hang on tight to keep from being catapulted overboard. Thoroughly chastened, I jibed and steered closer to shore. Still the seas continued to build, and now the wind began ripping at their crests, tearing away strands of icy spray. After plunging our bows deep into the descending side of several waves, I decided it was time to get off the water. Sailing in these conditions was too dangerous. I found the biggest pan I could and we pulled the boat up onto the ice.

We hauled the mainsail down and, using it for a windbreak, curled up on the ice between the bows. With open water in front of us, I was loath to stop sailing but since there was no choice for the moment, we decided we might as well get some badly needed rest. It was a relief to be out of the wind and spray, but now that we were immobile the cold began to extract its toll. My feet were like lifeless stumps by the time I roused myself and crawled out from under the sail – it took several minutes of jumping and running on the spot to revive the circulation. Firing up our tiny stove behind the windbreak, we cooked a meal of freeze-dried spaghetti, our first hot food in two days.

Thus restored, it seemed to us that conditions had improved somewhat, and at 4 P.M., we launched *Perception* into the foam-flecked waves. Visibility was so poor that we had no real idea where we were, beyond the fact that we had passed Bellot Strait and Somerset Island was somewhere to the right of us. Occasionally we would encounter the shore pack along the island's coastline and then tack back out to sea. The wind had veered around to the south southwest, and as conditions continued to deteriorate we were forced to douse the jib; Mike hauled in on the roller furling line from his perch near the mast on the trampoline. Under main alone, we charged ahead, the wind roaring and the air filled with a stinging mixture of snow and spindrift, the boat just barely under control.

A chain of ice stretching across the sound loomed out of the driving snow ahead, and without slowing much I sailed into the first opening I could find. It was filled with sharp brash ice and we wrestled *Perception* ahead until we were through to the other side. I aimed for the shore of Somerset Island and when we reached the ice fringe, we turned north once again and flew before the wind hoping to find an opening to land and safety, somewhere near Cape Granite. But the ice was forcing us back out into the sound.

With no way through the 10 km of shore ice and with weather conditions steadily worsening, our situation was becoming desperate. After a brief conference in which we had to shout to be heard above the storm, we decided to seek the relative safety of a large ice platform near the rim of the shore pack.

In the distance ahead, we were just able to make out what seemed to be a suitable floe, a massive piece of multi-year ice about the size of a hockey rink. As we approached, Mike shouted back to me, "This baby'll be around for another few winters." It did look good and solid so we dragged *Perception* aboard and struggled to haul down the main as it tried to flog itself to death in the wind. It was about 6:45 P.M.

The best spot to set up camp seemed to be in the lee of a meter-high slab of rafted ice on the main pan; the wind was too strong for us to risk erecting the tent on the trampoline as we always did when out on the ice. We pulled the boat over to the ice wall and began assembling our little dome, the wind trying all the while to rip it from our hands. We had the frame together and were ready to begin clipping on the nylon inner shell when a particularly violent gust tore the fabric out of our numbed fingers. For a heart-stopping instant I watched as our only shelter began tumbling across the ice toward the sea. Mike lunged after it and by some miracle managed to hold on. We finally got the tent organized with the main sail underneath to prevent ice melt and lots of equipment inside to keep it from blowing away. Then we collected what ice slabs we could and raised and enlarged our wind break.

It was nearly 9:00 by the time we felt we had the situation under control and could crawl into the tent to wait out the storm. I slid a tape into the Walkman and with the sound of Whitney Houston in the tiny loudspeakers competing with the groaning and grinding of the ice and the shrieking of the wind, I began to update my journal. Soon there was the comforting smell of paraffin in the air: Mike had lit the candle lantern and was busy trying to get the stove going. The prospect of a hot meal made our situation seem considerably less bleak.

I had written two and a half pages and was deep in thought trying to recall the details of the previous day's events when I heard Mike's voice, as if from a distance, "Jeff, the pan is cracking up!"

Looking up in mid-sentence, I thought he must be joking.

"Look for yourself! There's a crack right outside the tent door!"

I dropped my notebook and jerked on my dry-suit boots to follow Mike outside. As I emerged into the flying snow I saw to my horror that our big pan had broken into a dozen small pieces, each now moving independently in the swell and drifting slowly away from its neighbour. By the time I'd turned around, the back of our tent was in the water. If we didn't move quickly, we'd lose most of the equipment we depended upon for survival. I began frantically hauling our gear out and passing it to Mike, who stuffed it into waterproof bags and stowed it as quickly as he could aboard *Perception*.

The wind had reached a howling 70 km/h, blasting the snow at us almost horizontally. Together we lifted the bucking tent out of the rising water and fought it over to the boat and onto the tramp. While Mike struggled to lash it in place with ice-stiffened ropes, I began loading gear back inside to weigh it down. It seemed to work, and the tent and our gear appeared to be safe, for the moment.

But what were we to do now? We had no clear idea how far we were from land; certainly we couldn't see it in the darkness, fog and swirling snow. Worse, the postage stamp of ice we were on was already awash and was being blown slowly but surely out into the open water of the sound, where the storm was at its full fury and where it would be impossible for us to survive for long.

Our first thought was to try to move *Perception* to one of the larger pieces of our fractured pan. But a few minutes' scouting told us that none of the pieces was big enough to offer security. Our only option seemed to be to haul the boat as deep into the pack ice as possible, counting on the ice around us to prevent us from being blown into open water, and to protect us from the worst of the storm.

We would have to hurry, before the gaps opening in the ice around us became so wide that we couldn't safely cross them. First we had to flatten the tent and tie it down over the gear inside, to prevent it from ripping apart in the wind. That done, we paused for a moment to catch our breath and force down some high-energy food before getting to the grim business of dragging *Perception* over the heaving ice pans in the darkness and blinding snow.

In that moment it occurred to me that we were experiencing precisely the worst-case scenario my father and I had discussed months earlier: being blown offshore in a gale with no way of getting back. It was something we had decided must be avoided at all cost, because the consequences would likely be fatal.

On a count of three, Mike and I shoved the boat into the open water where our tent had so recently stood, and then hauled her onto the neighboring pan. For the next desperate two hours we pushed, shoved, dragged, cursed and cajoled her across the ice, weaving our way around widening leads of open water. But even as we crept toward the distant, invisible shore, the furious wind was reaching deeper into the pack, spreading it slowly out into the sound. It was a waking nightmare.

Finally, well after midnight, we decided we must stop. The storm seemed to be abating somewhat, and we were by now at least 2 km into the shore pack. Exhausted, we hauled *Perception* up onto the largest pan we could find. It was only about 10 by 15 m in extent, but this deep in the pack we felt reasonably sure it would be safe enough, and we badly needed rest. We reassembled the tent and climbed inside. I set my alarm for 3:30 A.M. and put it in my hat, but it was an unnecessary precaution: I found it impossible to sleep. Well before dawn, I crawled out to survey the ice. The wind was high, but no more than a Force 7 — about 60 km/h — and the pack around us seemed to be holding together. I crept back into my wet sleeping bag and finally managed to drift into unconsciousness for a couple of hours.

At 6:00 A.M. Mike and I were both awakened by a change in the intensity of sounds around us; the wind had piped up and the gusts were slamming against us with such violence we feared that *Perception* would be skidded off the pan. We looked outside into the driving snow and though the boat seemed safe enough for the moment, we saw with sinking hearts that the pack around us had begun to disperse, leaving us unprotected on our raft of ice. Land was nowhere to be seen.

For the next hour the wind continued to build until it was once again blowing a full gale. Our position was rapidly becoming untenable. Exhausted and badly frightened, we crawled out into the snow. I retrieved one of our paddles that had blown off the tramp and jammed it under the hull to immobilize it. As I did so, the boat suddenly slipped forward several inches. She was sliding off!

I shouted a warning to Mike and he began throwing equipment into our waterproof bags while I held on to *Perception*. By now, little waves were licking at the ice around us as the pack continued to disperse. Preparing for the worst, we struggled into our full flotation suits, slipped a food pouch inside and tucked our deflated Sea Seat flotation platforms into our belts. Then we frantically lashed everything down to the boat. I had the eerie feeling that I was watching all of this in a movie, that it was someone else's dream that was about to end in disaster, someone else who was about to pay the supreme price for challenging the elements.

In an adrenaline-charged flash of memory, I remembered the conversation I'd had in 1986 in Calgary with Pete Jess, ice specialist with Jessco. It had been a long talk, but there was one specific piece of advice that now seemed terribly important.

"You should take along a couple of mountaineering ice screws," he'd said. "They weigh practically nothing, and you never know when they might come in handy."

A little skeptical, I'd nonetheless taken his advice, and all last summer and this, two eight-inch, cast aluminum screws designed to secure a mountain climber's rope in ice had nestled unused at the bottom of the starboard hull of the boat.

I fumbled to unfasten the watertight access hatch on the hull and fished them out. In minutes, we'd worked them well into the ice and tied *Perception* down. For the moment, she was safe. Still trembling from our exertions, Mike and I began to weigh our options.

Trying to sail in these conditions would be suicide. But there was no longer any question of hauling the boat from pan to pan as we had last night — the pack had dispersed too much. In any case, we were no longer sure in which direction the land lay, or how far we had drifted in the night. Staying where we were seemed out of the question as well. Already waves were breaking over our pan, and the seas were continuing to mount. We had to sail, if only to reach a bigger, more stable pan to cling to while the storm blew itself out.

Fighting with frozen, ice-encrusted lines, we reefed the main right down and started to haul on the halyard. Immediately, the sail began flogging violently in the wind; the mast was wrenched back and forth with such force that I felt sure it would snap.

I shouted to Mike over the deafening pandemonium of ice, wind and waves and the machine-gun crackling of flailing sail cloth. "She's starting to tear. We'll have to haul her down." We looked at each other, realizing our last option was gone.

With the mainsail lashed once again to its boom, we hung on grimly to *Perception* as the waves tossed our little island of ice. I found our small emergency locator transmitter and attached its antenna, though Mike and I were both thinking how futile it would be to turn on the homing device. Nothing could fly in this weather — we were beyond rescue. I have never felt closer to death than in those minutes.

Then the single word, scarcely audible above the screaming wind: "Land!"

I followed the line of Mike's extended arm and there, just visible through the snow and spray, was the faint shadow of land! And we were being blown toward it! It was Pressure Point thrusting into the sound ahead of us. It seemed a miracle.

With each passing minute, the rugged outline of land became more distinct. I prayed fervently that our ice pan would hold together until we'd hit the main pack, and that the ice screws would hold *Perception*.

Walls of water were breaking over our tiny island as we rode the two-story seas to their summits and down the other side. The ice seemed to be melting away beneath us, our platform shrinking steadily. We loosened the ice screws and pointed *Perception*'s nose into the shrieking wind to ease the strain on the lines holding her fast. But then the pan twisted and we had to do it all over again — and again and again, each time struggling to tie and untie knots in the frozen lines with wooden fingers.

Slowly, meter by meter, we were being blown into Ashton Bay until we finally smashed into the shore pack. I checked my watch. It was 11:15 A.M. As we waited, too numb to move, the ice slowly filled in behind us, forming a continuous pack that rose and fell like the undulating belly of some enormous, gray sea monster.

*"IT HAD BEEN A YEAR IN WHICH
SUMMER HAD NEVER REALLY COME TO
THE ARCTIC."*

Chapter 10

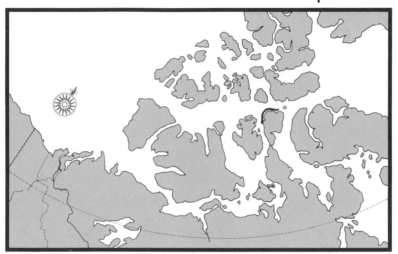

Still we could not rest — we had 2 km of bucking, grinding ice to cross before we would be on shore and truly safe. It was not going to be easy, but at least the end of our ordeal was in sight. I retrieved a lunch packet and we wolfed down some dried fruit and chocolate. Then we released *Perception* from her bonds and began to push, grateful now for the assistance of a powerful tail wind.

At mid-afternoon, with the wind still howling in unabated fury, we hauled *Perception* up on the shore near the head of Ashton Bay. Feeble with exhaustion and trembling with relief, we dropped to our knees and kissed the snow-covered ground. It was wonderful to be alive.

Now that we'd stopped moving, we began to feel the effects of the cold, and so we set about erecting our tent as quickly as we could, building a chest-high wall of snow blocks for protection from the wind. As we were unloading some of our gear from *Perception*, a chart was torn from my hands and blown away up the hill. I stumbled after it, but in vain: it was gone forever. At any other time such a loss would have been a catastrophe, but now I scarcely gave it a second thought. All that mattered was that we had survived. Mike found his cognac bottle and offered me a swig; I gratefully accepted and we wearily carried on with the business of setting up camp.

With the storm still raging about us, we spent part of the next day raising and strengthening the snow wall around our tent. Inside, we dried, cleaned and organized the gear we'd stowed so haphazardly the day before. I spent much of the afternoon catching up on my journal. Mike told me that all through yesterday he'd been wishing desperately he'd been able to scratch a small note to his parents, to tell them that if he was to meet his end, he was doing what he loved best – exploring. These heart-felt words reminded me how close we had been to losing our lives.

Sharing the prolonged terror of the storm seemed to bring Mike and me closer together and I never again questioned his commitment to the expedition. Nor, I think, did he ever again question my ability to lead it.

The following morning, September 1, I was awake at 6:00 for our regular radio schedule, but was unable to raise either Resolute or Cambridge Bay. The weather was still poor, so we decided to recuperate for another day before getting underway again. We ate a hot dinner at 6:30 and were in bed by 9:00 in the comfort of our snow-walled shelter.

Light winds, overcast skies with good visibility and an outside temperature of $-2°$C greeted us the next morning, but once again my attempt to keep our morning radio schedule was unsuccessful. If we didn't reach them soon, they would send out a search plane.

We started up the stove and cooked an enormous breakfast of oatmeal and freeze-dried chicken stew, but even though we were much restored in body and spirit, getting ourselves and the boat ready to move proved to be an arduous task. Our boots, our dry-suits, our flotation overalls all were frozen stiff, and it was none too pleasant trying to get them on. Everything on the boat was frozen, too. Every line had to be twisted and manipulated until it became flexible. The trampoline had to be pounded and scraped to remove a thick covering of ice. Even the tent poles were frozen together; each joint had to be warmed by hand before it could be pulled apart, and it took still more time to beat the ice out of the tent itself and its fly. Then the stiffened material had to be rolled and forced through the little storage hatch in the hull. Finally we broke down our snow wall and pulled *Perception* around to face the ice pack, strapping on her plastic runners.

Leaning on one of her wings to catch my breath, I told Mike confidently, "Well, the hardest part of the day is over. It's all downhill from here."

Again I was wrong. Ahead of us was the most physically exhausting trial of the voyage so far.

For two days, the storm had piled ice into the bay, choking it completely and leaving us 8 km from open water in the sound. This had the potential to be a very serious problem for us because this late in the season, every day, every hour counted if we were to make it through the passage before winter barred the way.

I had gauged it might take four to six hours of hauling to get *Perception* across the pack ice that now completely choked Ashton Bay and out to the open water in Peel Sound. In the end, we pushed and hauled for fourteen hours and had covered just 2 km when we were forced to stop for the night, too weary to go on.

The ice we were crossing was rafted into a jungle of jagged, sharp-edged slabs and there was no easy way through. *Perception*'s hulls were taking a vicious beating and so were we; the 5 cm of snow we'd had overnight was just enough to conceal the open water leads between the pans, which meant that Mike and I were continually crashing through into the freezing water. To make any progress at all we had to adopt a technique that involved Mike rolling over the thinnest of the ice until he reached a solid pan. Then, with him pulling on a rope and me pushing the boat from the rear when there was solid footing, we slowly moved ahead. It felt like trying to keep afloat on quicksand.

By late evening we'd reached an area of slush that slowed our snail-like progress even further and it was clear that we were not going to reach open water that day. The idea of spending another night out on the ice terrified us, and so we began pushing the boat back in toward the shore. Since we'd been following the shoreline of the bay for most of the day, that meant a course change of about 30° to the right.

We were in deepening twilight when the boat suddenly slipped out of our grip and lurched sideways to come crashing down on a jagged block of multi-year ice. There was a loud crunch and an ominous tearing sound. We both stumbled to the front of the hull Mike had been hauling and there, staring back at us, was a hole big enough to push a fist through.

I cursed our wretched luck. The hole could be repaired, but the job would take hours and it was fast getting dark. On the other hand, if we continued to push through the slush toward land, the hull would fill with water, which could then freeze and become impossible to remove.

We pushed on to the nearest pan big enough to support *Perception* and took stock; the wind was light and blowing steadily on shore, and though we were still too far from land for comfort, we were reasonably close to a range of hills that would to some extent protect us should the wind veer around to the east.

In an agony of frustration, we decided we must remain out on the ice once again. The plain fact was that after fourteen hours, we were too exhausted to carry on even if we'd wanted to. It was well after midnight before we could crawl into our sleeping bags; my whole body ached as if I'd been thrown down a flight of stairs.

My alarm woke me at 6 A.M. for our radio schedule, but once again there was nobody there. Either that, or our transmitter was no longer working — a disturbing thought that made our sense of isolation all the more palpable. I rolled over and slept for another three hours while a strong west wind buffeted the tent and sleet rattled against the thin fabric. After a dreary breakfast, we crawled outside and began repairing the hole in *Perception*'s starboard bow. The fiberglass repair material had to be painstakingly heated over our little stove and then quickly applied in the extreme cold outside — it was a tediously slow procedure.

While we were waiting for our repair to dry, I pulled out the radio and tried once again to reach Polar Shelf. This time, they could hear us, and there was unsettling news. John Bockstoce, in the wisdom of his vast experience, had decided it was time to stop for the summer and *Belvedere* was heading back to Tuktoyaktuk. This was not what I wanted to hear.

It was early evening by the time we were ready once again to resume the misery of hauling the boat over the ice. We continued on up the shoreline of the bay until at 10:30, with darkness upon us and the wind still onshore, we found a large pan. We set up camp and remained there uneasily through the night.

Early morning found us once again miserably dragging *Perception* across the ragged ice, our spirits as low as they'd been all season. We hadn't bothered to stow the tent, preferring instead to let it ride on the tramp so that we wouldn't have to go through the bother of putting it up that night. It seemed as though we'd never escape from this ice-choked hell.

At mid-morning we stopped to scout the way ahead. The

winds were light and the sea beneath us seemed relatively calm. Mike was already out ahead on the ice and I was preparing to join him when I heard him shout, "Polar bear! Grab the binoculars."

My own first thought was, "The hell with binoculars, get the shotgun." I fished it out of the tent, and then returned for the flares for good measure. By now Mike was back at the boat to get his cameras. It was only tracks he'd seen, but they were huge, he said, and very fresh.

Armed with our cameras and guns, we walked back to where Mike had seen the tracks and began to follow them toward a house-sized slab of blue ice that projected skyward about 50 m from the boat. They were indeed abnormally large tracks, almost double the length of Mike's footprint. Slowly and very gingerly we approached the ice slab and peered around the corner. The bear was nowhere to be seen, but its tracks told the story: the animal had circled almost completely around us without our knowing it, before taking off toward land.

An hour later we had reached the outer rim of the pack ice, and at long last it seemed we would be able to resume sailing. We stowed the tent and generally made *Perception* ready for sea; we began pushing her over the last 100 m, in newly formed ice that was not quite thick enough to consistently support us. We fell through often, but nothing could discourage us now. Soon we were in mulch ice, falling, stumbling, hauling and dragging the boat until we were once again, to our unspeakable relief, in open water. Mike and I exchanged high fives with as much gusto as we had left in us.

We immediately got underway in the light westerly winds. *Perception* seemed sluggish and we raised the chute to try to get a little more speed out of her as we approached the immense rock outcropping called Pressure Point. I let out a whoop of pleasure that startled Mike and then made him smile: it was such a joy to be moving at last and to be seeing new landscape after being trapped in Ashton Bay for nearly five days.

We were now entering Barrow Strait at lat. 74°N, and the temperature seemed to plummet as we rounded the massive, blunt face of Limestone Island. All our lines were stiff with ice, and I could feel the sweat begin to freeze on the back of my pile suit. We donned our Mustang floater overalls, but still we were cold. I jibed for Cape Anne in the distance off to starboard, hoping now that we'd be able to reach Cunningham Inlet well along the northern coast of Somerset Island, before stopping for the day. The wind was building and several times I alerted Mike to be ready to drop the chute.

Something, however, was wrong with the way *Perception* was handling. I began to look her over as we skimmed along. Finally it dawned on me: she was lying far too low in the water.

Mike spun open the cargo hatch on the port hull and found it half full of water. He dug out our little hand-operated bilge pump and began using it, but the sea was pouring in as fast as he pumped it out. With a despairing look at me, he moved over to check the starboard hull. It was nearly full. We were sinking!

We tacked in toward Cape Anne, aiming for a small island just offshore. The wind drove *Perception* right up onto the beach and we jumped into the foam to pull her ashore. She wouldn't budge. It took 300 strokes of the hand pump to clear enough water from the starboard hull for us to be able to move her; with an enormous effort we hauled her up the beach and removed the plugs behind the rudders to drain the hulls. As we looked her over carefully, we could see that we had a major repair job to do, patching up the damage done during our days of purgatory in Ashton Bay.

The next day, September 5, the wind was blowing at 70 km/h, creating a wind chill equal to −30°C, and it was snowing hard. At 6 A.M. a series of particularly vicious gusts rousted us out of bed to build a snow wall to protect our fragile nylon dome. Before we could get outside, we had to spend some time clearing the drift that had all but covered the tent's entrance.

Later that afternoon, a Twin Otter responding to our radioed request flew out of Resolute Bay and across Barrow Strait to try to deliver epoxy repair material to patch up the damage to *Perception*'s hulls. My father and Peter Jess were on board.

The plane made several passes trying to find a suitable place to drop down on its tundra tires but the wind was creating obvious difficulties for the pilot. On the last pass, a downdraft forced the pilot right down to deck level with full throttle, and we thought for a terrifying moment that he was going to crash. After that, he headed back to Resolute.

The plane's narrow escape forced me to face the facts of our situation. Ice conditions were bad and getting worse, and we could expect the temperature to continue falling. Our dry-suits and boat were both torn and leaking from the jagged ice. Our own strength had been sapped by forty days of effort. For a day and a half as the storm raged around us, I weighed our chances. Finally, with tears of frustration in my eyes, I made the painful decision to interrupt the voyage where we were.

It was another day before the wind had moderated enough for the plane to return to rescue us from Cape Anne. Mike and I lowered *Perception*'s mast, removed her sails and trampoline, generally battening her down as well as we could, knowing she could face extremes of −50°C temperatures and 160-km/h winds during the long winter ahead. The big polar bear tracks we saw in the snow on the morning of our departure were a source of added worry; the animals had been known to destroy snowmobiles in their search for morsels of edible material.

Reflecting on the summer's events while waiting in Resolute

for our plane south, I felt we had reason to be proud of our accomplishment. We had managed to cover 1,600 km of ice-choked waters in what has been traditionally recognized as the most difficult section of the passage. Other vessels hadn't been so fortunate.

Vagabond II had left Gjoa Haven a few days after our own departure but wasn't able to slip through the ice jam in James Ross Strait. They waited there until the end of September before turning around and motoring the 200 km back to Gjoa.

John Bockstoce in *Belvedere* left Tuktoyaktuk and managed to get nearly as far east as *Vagabond* before being blocked by the ice and returning to Tuk for the winter.

British sailor David Cowper told us his own story in Resolute. We met him for tea in the kitchen of an outfitter's lodge, where he stood out as probably the only person in the eastern Arctic to be wearing a tie. Though still a young man, David had already completed three solo circumnavigations and was now attempting his fourth, which would include an east-west transit of the passage. He'd motored into Lancaster Sound and down Prince Regent Inlet to Creswell Bay in his converted 12-m lifeboat in the summer of 1986, before being beset by ice for the winter. When he returned to the boat the following spring, he found it had been made full of holes and was half-filled with water. While we had been struggling through the ice toward Gjoa Haven, he'd been spending his time repairing his vessel, getting her seaworthy and waiting for the ice to open in the bay. Finally in late August, a lead did open and he followed it 20 km to a dead end. He was forced to return to Creswell Bay and again prepare his boat for winter after having traveled only 40 km all season.

It had been a year in which summer had never really come to the Arctic, and David expressed astonishment at the distance we'd been able to cover in *Perception*. The frank admiration of this extraordinary man was some consolation for not quite having completed the passage.

Perception had proved herself to be the ideal vessel for our journey. When conditions were good, she fairly flew over the water and though it was by no means pleasant hauling her over ice, we'd managed to cover nearly 50 km of "hard water" doing just that. We left full of confidence and eager to return to finish the job.

YEAR THREE — 1988

July 26 – August 17

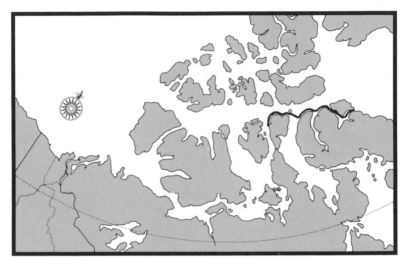

"THE ANIMALS SEEMED AS CURIOUS ABOUT US AS WE WERE ABOUT THEM."

Chapter 11

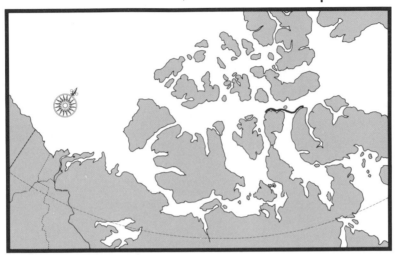

On July 21, 1988, I awoke in Toronto at 6 A.M. The fast-talking morning man on the radio told me it was 29°C and that a multi-vehicle accident had already been reported on the turgid river of steel known as the Don Valley Parkway.

Fourteen hours later my father, Mike and I were stepping off a plane into a foggy, 5°C chill in Resolute, accompanied by a three-man film crew who would be recording the final leg of our passage for a television documentary. The sturdy 737 that carried us from Iqaluit (formerly Frobisher Bay) on the southern extremity of Baffin Island was one of the workhorses of the Arctic: a kind of modern tramp steamer — half cargo hold, half passenger space. There were several American tourists aboard who had tried to get into Resolute the day before, only to be turned back by bad weather. Now they'd finally arrived, after having spent twenty hours in the air over the past two days. This is travel in the north.

We spent the night in the Narwhal Hotel near the airport, a

two-story, semi-circular building that is the best-equipped such
facility and staging location in the high Arctic. The next day we
stuffed the expedition's gear into the cargo hold of a chartered
Twin Otter along with the TV crew's tents, generator, cameras
and spare parts. The six of us — me, Mike, Dad and the film
crew — squeezed in behind the gear for the flight to Cape Anne
and *Perception*. On the way, we planned a stopover at Beechey
Island, a place of considerable historical interest, and one of
significance for my father and me.

As we lifted off the runway, we could see the parallel lines of
truck tracks defacing the delicate dove-colored land around the
settlement like a subway vandal's scribbles, unhappy evidence
of technological man's intrusion into the pristine northern
environment.

Moments later we were over Barrow Strait, where we could
see ice floes crowded along the north shore. Wellington
Channel, to the east of Resolute and now straight ahead of us,
was jammed solid, but we could see leads along the southern
fringe of the pack and pans were breaking off and edging their
way south into the strait. And then Gibraltar-like Beechey
Island was in sight, and we began our descent as our pilot, an
Arctic veteran, searched the tilting horizon for a reasonably flat
place on which to set down the Twin Otter on its fat tundra
tires.

We touched down with a crunch at the end of the narrow
strip of gravel that connects Beechey to the land mass of Devon
Island at low water, and rolled uphill toward the steep cliffs,
finally turning to taxi slowly over to the island's famous grave
site. While the camera crew set about organizing their
equipment, Dad and I walked over to the three wooden
headboards that marked the graves of crewmen of Sir John
Franklin, men who had died during the winter of 1846 and were
buried at the expedition's first shore quarters. This site had
been discovered in 1850 by one of the many expeditions sent

out in search of Franklin and his men, and it has changed little since. Franklin's mute stone cairn remains — he left no message in it — as do remnants of a large wooden structure, built to house naval stores in 1854 by Commander Pullen of HMS *North Star*. Nearby there were pieces of the hull and rudder of the yacht *Mary*, a little 12-ton vessel left at Cape Spencer on Devon Island by Commander John Ross in 1850, in hopes it would serve the survivors of the Franklin expedition should they find it. It was later towed to Beechey by Commander Pullen.

I reread the memorial sent here by the grieving Lady Franklin and erected by Captain Leopold McClintock during the privately financed search expedition that was eventually, in 1857-58, to unlock the secret of what happened to Franklin and his men.

TO THE MEMORY OF
FRANKLIN,
CROZIER, FITZJAMES
AND ALL THEIR GALLANT BROTHER OFFICERS
AND FAITHFUL COMPANIONS WHO HAVE
SUFFERED AND PERISHED IN THE CAUSE OF
SCIENCE AND THE SERVICE OF THEIR COUNTRY.
THIS TABLET IS ERECTED NEAR THE SPOT WHERE
THEY PASSED THEIR FIRST ARCTIC WINTER, AND
WHENCE THEY ISSUED FORTH TO CONQUER
DIFFICULTIES OR TO DIE. IT COMMEMORATES
THE GRIEF OF THEIR ADMIRING COUNTRYMEN
AND FRIENDS; AND THE ANGUISH, SUBDUED BY
FAITH, OF HER WHO HAS LOST, IN THE HEROIC
LEADER OF THE EXPEDITION, THE MOST
DEVOTED AND AFFECTIONATE HUSBAND
"AND SO HE BRINGETH THEM UNTO THE
HEAVEN WHERE THEY WOULD BE."
1855

The marble tablet is placed at the base of a stone cenotaph erected during the last and largest of the Royal Navy's Franklin search missions, undertaken by five Royal Navy ships under the command of Sir Edward Belcher. By all accounts Belcher was one of the most incompetent officers ever to visit the Arctic, and in 1853 he abandoned four of his ships and fled home on transport vessels that had arrived at Beechey Island to resupply his expedition. His flagship, which he had deserted in the ice in Wellington Channel, managed to find its own way into the North Atlantic the following summer where it was found drifting by American whalers.

Dad and I walked further down the rocky beach to where in 1978 we had set up camp during the first year of his expedition in search of the wreck of the *Breadalbane*. The three-masted barque had been one of the vessels sent out from England to resupply Belcher, and she'd been crushed in heavy pack ice shortly after arriving off Beechey Island in late August 1853. She sank in less than fifteen minutes. The quest for her remains using the most up-to-date side-scan sonar took three years, working frantically against time in the short summer season, and ended with the discovery of the perfectly preserved ship lying upright, spars still standing, in 300 m of water. In 1981, the year following the discovery, the expedition returned to photograph the vessel, now established as the world's northernmost shipwreck. Finally in 1983, we spent a month camped on the ice over the ship, making several fly-pasts with a small, remotely piloted submersible. A series of thrilling manned dives in a specially made suit retrieved the ship's wheel and other artifacts from the hulk.

It had been here at the Beechey Island ice camp in 1983 that I had first conceived of the idea of sailing the Northwest Passage. Being a part of the team that had found the *Breadalbane* had left me extremely interested in the stories of the Arctic explorers. I wanted to see with my own eyes the sights they'd described and share the experience of conquest and discovery.

My father had described the search for the *Breadalbane* in his book *The Land That Devours Ships*; as we climbed back aboard the Twin Otter, I fervently hoped it hadn't devoured our little vessel. We banked across Lancaster Sound toward Somerset Island. The sound was choked with pans of first-year ice, some of them several kilometers across, but as we approached the northern coast of the island the ice thinned until, along the shoreline, it looked as though we might be able to squeeze through. Looking down over Cunningham Inlet we could see ghostly white shapes gliding slowly across the mottled brown and green shallows. As we circled for a better look, we counted sixty beluga whales, swimming in pods of four to twelve.

Finally Cape Anne loomed ahead and I was seized anew by the anxiety that had plagued me all winter . . . would *Perception* be in sound condition after spending almost a year unattended and exposed to the elements on the open tundra? We'd secured her as best we could when we'd been forced to abandon her eleven months earlier, but neither Mike nor I needed to be reminded of the terrible fury of a winter storm this far north. There was certainly no guarantee that she would have survived intact.

Mike, on the other side of the plane, was the first to spot her. "I see her down there," he shouted. "She looks okay!"

The Twin Otter banked steeply and we made a slow circle around *Perception* before descending quickly for a remarkably smooth landing on the tundra. Mike and I were out of our seat belts in a flash, and it seemed an eternity before the pilot had shut down the engines and done his cockpit check prior to opening the door for us.

Once on the ground, we sprinted across to *Perception*. She really did seem all right. I slapped the battered yellow fiberglass of her starboard hull and there was a reassuring hollow echo. She looked wonderful. I planted a kiss on her nose.

We immediately set up camp, and while Dad got started on dinner, Mike and I flipped *Perception*'s hulls upside down to expose last year's ice punctures. The damage was considerable, but not nearly as bad as it had seemed to us in our exhausted state eleven months ago. Luckily, it was nothing we couldn't handle with the repair materials we'd brought with us. We got to work with sandpaper and epoxy resin, which was slow to stiffen in the gusting winds. The resin had a reddish tinge to it, making our repairs look hideous, but we kept at it.

Throughout most of the following day, July 24, we continued to work on the damaged hulls. By late afternoon we were ready to flip her upright again and begin reassembling the trampoline, the wings and the rigging. By dinner time, she was ready to launch, though the wind was too strong for sailing.

That evening, on the escarpment behind our campsite, Mike discovered the remnants of a Thule Eskimo encampment. We could see traces of five dwellings in the rock and whalebone that littered the ground. The ancient site afforded a clear view of the coast below, and looking down in the Arctic twilight we could see belugas sporting in the shallow water. It was a moment of pure enchantment. I was grateful to be in the high Arctic once again and wondered what the coming weeks held in store.

After a day of sea trials and taping with the TV crew, our voyage resumed in earnest, on July 26. Dad had flown south, and the film crew had returned to Resolute. We had a short day, sailing through waters relatively free of ice, east toward Cunningham Inlet. High winds forced us off the water by 7:00 P.M. and we pitched our tent on *Perception*'s trampoline. During the night the wind rose further to shriek in the rigging and tear at the nylon shell of our dome. In these conditions we weren't sure whether we'd pulled the boat far enough up the shore to be clear of the overnight high water mark, and so we were able to get very little sleep.

With the dawn, the wind moderated and there came low, gray clouds and a cold drizzle. By the time we were afloat again, the waves on Barrow Strait were white-capped and about a meter high and *Perception*, heavily laden with supplies, plunged through them sluggishly, showering us with stinging spray.

We reached the mouth of Cunningham Inlet in mid-afternoon, turning into its protected waters with relief, to see if we could locate the belugas we'd spotted from our aircraft three days earlier. It didn't take long; within minutes we were alongside a pod of ten, sailing straight downwind, ghost-like in the clear, blue-green water beneath our hulls. For a few minutes the whales seemed to accept our presence, and then they vanished as suddenly as they'd appeared. Farther into the inlet we intercepted another pod, but these ones sounded almost immediately and sped away. We must have frightened them.

By now, we could see the hills of the southern shoreline of the inlet quite clearly and were able to pick out a camp we knew must be the whale research station we'd been told about in Resolute. As we neared the beach, a three-wheeled motorbike carrying a big, bearded man raced across the tundra to greet us. We splashed ashore to meet Canadian research biologist Tom Smith, and before we'd pulled *Perception* out of the water we had an invitation to visit the scientists' camp and join them for dinner.

As we walked up the beach toward the station, we were transfixed by the sight of belugas swimming just offshore. Now and then they'd glide right up into the shallows and noisily thrash the water into foam and spray before heading back out into the depths of the inlet. It was difficult for Mike and me to turn our backs on this awe-inspiring scene when it came time to scale the 60-m escarpment below the camp.

The research station consisted of a wooden building about 3.5 by 5 m in extent, perched right on the cliff side, and two small tents. By Arctic standards, this seemed luxurious accommodation, given that there were just Tom and two other scientists, Tony Martin from Cambridge University and Cathy Frost, a biologist with the Alaska Fish and Game Department. They told us that for the past twelve years the place had been occupied each summer by specialists studying the behavior of the belugas. Each year some 1500 whales return to the shallow and relatively warm waters that make the inlet unique, to rub their bodies on the sandy bottom and remove the dead and yellowing outer layer of skin. The mature animals emerge from the process a snowy white.

As part of the study of the whales' migrations, Tony had recently strapped a small radio transmitter to the back of one of the animals — not an easy task, he assured us — and it was being tracked by a satellite that relayed information on the animal's whereabouts to his lab in Cambridge, England. By a remarkable coincidence, Mike had seen and photographed a beluga with a curious orange package on its back just two days earlier, at Cape Anne. It had to be the same animal, because it was the first time a beluga had ever been banded in this way. Tony was ecstatic; the placing of the whale in an exact location at a precise time would enable him to verify his satellite fixes back at Cambridge.

Two whales had accidentally beached themselves in the delta of a small river near the research station that morning, and now that the tide had gone out, they were unable to return to the sea. For the scientists, this presented a rare opportunity to tag, measure, determine sex and examine the creatures at close range — a beaching like this might occur only once every three or four years. Mike and I excitedly followed along as the five of us forded several small river channels and traversed a number of sand bars before finding the stranded animals.

The first whale we reached was about 6 m long and pure white, and so, we were told, must have been at least seven years old. It was lying in about a foot of water, on what must have been an uncomfortable bed of rocks. We approached it with caution, although it seemed to have exhausted itself in its thrashing attempts to return to the sea, and was resting quietly. I reached out to touch its skin: it had the feel and texture of week-old Jell-O. The flesh was deeply scarred in several places.

As the scientists carried out their examination, taking a small flesh sample and checking the animal's sex (a delicate task involving reaching inside the genital slit), it would occasionally muster the energy to resume its fruitless effort to escape to the sea, thrashing violently while we stumbled back in hasty retreat.

Having established that this specimen was a female, we moved to where the second whale was stranded. This one, also a female, was gray, and only about one-third the size of its companion. The scientists estimated its age at three months, and it was whining and trembling between bouts of desperate thrashing movements, clearly traumatized by the beaching. We could all feel her distress with poignant clarity, and Tom decided we'd try to get her back into the water. With an enormous effort, the four of us managed to spin her around, and began towing her backward into deeper water. Tom and I pulled on her tail and the others hauled away at her black-fringed flukes. Slowly, we were able to inch the enormous creature back into deeper water until, with one final thrashing movement, she was afloat and quickly swam off. The other whale, at about a tonne, was simply too heavy for us to budge, and so she would have to take her chances with marauding polar bears until the tide returned.

Back at the research station, we enjoyed a hot dinner with our new friends before returning to *Perception* for the night. Mike and I rolled out our bivy sacks on the pebble beach by the water's edge, and in the all-night twilight we were able to watch and listen to the whales frolicking no more than 10 m from where we lay. As they moved in groups along the shore, their heads, backs and finally their tails would break the surface in a graceful undulating motion, and we could hear their deep exhalations. Occasionally one would spy-hop out of the water, rising vertically until its enormous white head and tiny, obsidian-black eyes were several feet in the air, and then falling back into the sea with a tremendous splash. The animals seemed to be as curious about us as we were about them. At times there were so many whales that the sea looked like the rapids in a river, as the great beasts kept the water boiling with their playful thrashing. They have sometimes been called sea canaries, and it was easy to tell why: their chirps and whistles kept us entertained long into the night.

Although we were up at 8:00, it was after 1:00 before we could tear ourselves away from the wonderful tableau before us and launch *Perception*. Then we spent the next hour and a half with me sailing the boat back and forth along the shoreline so Mike could try to capture the boat and a breaching whale in the same frame. But we were unlucky and there was no *National Geographic* shot for Mike this day.

As we crossed the threshold of Cunningham Inlet to the light, fluky winds in Barrow Strait, we could see right to the sandy bottom, where long brown strands of kelp streamed horizontally in the current. Brightly colored jellyfish drifted by as our boat indolently rode the low swell, the wind too weak to fill her sails. We napped, ate and eventually, out of sheer boredom, took to the paddles. Late in the afternoon we spotted a huge bearded seal basking on a small ice pan. We paddled toward him as quietly as we could, and it wasn't until we were within about a boat length that he slid his 180-kg bulk off the ice and dove for safety. An hour later we decided to call it a day and set up camp, hoping the next morning would bring a fair wind.

We paddled in to the shore and I caught a glimpse of something white moving slowly against the predominantly brown shoreline. Even without binoculars, the power and speed of its movements told us it could only be a polar bear — our first sighting of the season. As usual, Mike was more sanguine about the thought of sharing a stretch of shoreline with one of these animals than I was. We watched as it followed an erratic course along the fringe of the beach. Mike said he thought it must be looking for food. In any case, he said, the big bears seldom double back on their own tracks, preferring to keep moving in the same direction. Thus reassured, I agreed to set up camp. We made sure the shotgun was loaded and close at hand, and when we rolled out our bivy sacks on the tundra we placed a can of anti-bear Mace between us — a new wrinkle in our elaborate defence system. I felt very exposed, but I was also very tired and soon fell asleep.

Though a light rain had begun sometime during the night, I slept soundly until 7:30 when I awoke with a start, genuinely surprised that I'd made it through the night without being molested by our polar bear. There was still no wind, so we snuggled back down into our bags and caught another two hours' sleep. By noon we'd breakfasted on granola bars and packed the boat. The wind was strong enough for us to push off from shore. During the night the shoreline had become cluttered with ice pans about the size of our boat and we had to push through these to get to open water. When we did, I looked back and could see the polar bear stretched out quietly on a low ridge about 2 km from where we'd camped. He must have spent the night there, within easy striking distance of our bivouac.

The wind remained light and from the west, and since we were headed due east, we tacked back and forth downwind, trying to keep *Perception* close to her best point of sail. Soon we hoisted the 325-square-foot spinnaker. It was the first time the big yellow kite with its oversized maple leaf had been flown since early spring, when I'd used it training in the Florida Gulf Stream. There was a shower of Florida sand and bits of shell as it bellied out with a snap. *Perception* surged ahead powerfully.

The sun had made a rare appearance, and the day had become quite warm. For the first time I could remember, we were able to sail for several hours without wearing gloves. As Prince Leopold Island came into view, the wind picked up and really set the rudders humming. We carried on like this, making excellent time, until about 9:30, when the wind dropped, and then died altogether with typical Arctic fickleness. We were both chilled through and ravenously hungry, but we were reluctant to paddle for shore since the odds were good that the wind would pipe up again.

Instead, while Mike took the tiller, I set up our cookstove on the tramp, filled a pot with water and began boiling it for soup. We had to jibe once during this process; Mike held the pot on the stove while I carried the spinnaker across the front of the boat. When the water boiled, I scooped some of it up in our mugs and added powdered vegetable soup. We enjoyed that while our beef stroganoff dinner was rehydrating in its foil packets. With our first few mouthfuls of hot food, we felt like new men. And then, to make the meal all the more memorable, a pod of about ten belugas swept past us, heading west toward Cunningham Inlet in a rhythmic series of breaches and shallow dives among the ice floes. It was a stunningly beautiful sight.

The wind picked up a little and we ghosted along toward the barren gray rock of Cape Clarence. It was almost midnight before the cape's massive cliffs came in view. The water ahead of us was choked with an almost continuous covering of ice, but the floes were separated widely enough for us to pick our way between them. Then the wind died almost completely and we slipped along under the chute looking for an opening in the ice that would allow us to land for the night.

When we reached the tip of the cape, we found ourselves confronted by a wall of ice that was being driven toward us on an eddy created in the merging currents of Prince Regent Inlet and Lancaster Sound. It was a frightening sight — millions of tonnes of shifting, grinding ice inexorably bearing down on us — and we pulled out the paddles and plied them with a vengeance, heading back in the direction from which we'd come, searching for shelter in a small bay we'd passed. As hard as we paddled, the ice kept gaining on us until at the last moment we were able to dodge behind a large land-fast floe to safety. When we caught our breath, we hauled *Perception* up on the beach and, climbing a 5-m block of rafted ice, watched the floes pile into the bay behind us. We wondered whether we were going to get trapped in here, but after more than fourteen hours at sea and 80 km under our hulls, we were too tired to care. Once again we slept on the beach without bothering to unpack our tent.

My alarm woke us for our radio schedule at 9:00, and while I reported our position, Mike scouted the ice. He didn't have far to look — a strong tide was pushing thc floes right up onto the beach where we'd slept. It looked as though we were going to be blockaded. With visions of last year's nightmare in Ashton Bay still vivid in our minds, we shook off our fatigue and in an hour we were pushing *Perception* down the beach to meet the sea at low tide.

Our shallow little bay was busy with drifting bergs ranging in size from a small truck to a large house, and getting *Perception* underway without damaging her was a lot like trying to merge with freeway traffic from a standing start. We'd no sooner raised the mainsail than we found ourselves on a collision course with a towering ice overhang that threatened to snag the sail and snap the mast. Mike fended us off with a paddle as we

shot past and, with one or two more hair-raising tacks, we left
the ice behind and emerged into open water.

The wind was too strong and conditions were too unsettled
for us to consider the 60-km crossing of Prince Regent Inlet – a
day's voyage across open water – and so we aimed *Perception*
for Prince Leopold Island, about an hour's sail ahead. We were
both perched on the windward wing, drenched in spray, as the
boat hurtled toward the limestone cliffs. We landed where a
broad river valley opened to the sea, and dragged our vessel
high up above the waterline, planning to wait until conditions
were favorable for a crossing.

Prince Leopold is a haven for millions of sea birds and, as we
were to discover, has a harsh beauty all its own. We knew that
there was a research station here somewhere on the heights
300 m above sea level, and as soon as we'd secured the boat, we
set out to find it. We followed the boulder-strewn bed of the
cataract, shifting part way up to a snow-covered central ridge
that divided the water into two fast-flowing, icy streams. Red
snow algae dusted the ground beneath our feet, and at the head
of the river valley we discovered a brilliant red moss on the
rocks beneath the snow.

As we reached the island plateau, we spotted the wooden
windscreen of one of the bird observers, just at the brink of the
escarpment. Huddled behind it was John Shadon, from the
Bedford Institute of Oceanography in Nova Scotia. His
specialty was the kittiwake, a small gray and white ocean-rang-
ing gull that builds its nest of grass, moss, seaweed and excretia
against the sheer rock cliffs of Prince Leopold and other islands
in the northern archipelago. In the winter, they range as far
south as the Mediterranean and North Africa.

The view from John's shelter was breathtaking, with
thousands of the kittiwakes clinging noisily to the rock wall that
rose straight out of the white-capped ocean far below. As many

murres or guillemots busily competed for space on what little level ground was provided by the narrow rock ledges.

We stayed, talking and watching the birds for an hour, and then followed John back to the camp he shared with four other researchers doing population counts and studying the island's birds. Project leader David Nettleship had studied here for more than a dozen years. He described how each summer the murres return to the island with the same mate and find exactly the same nesting place on the cliffs in which to hatch their brood. At the end of the season the chicks, still unable to fly, float down to the ocean far below to begin a slow drift for 5000 km on the currents out of Lancaster Sound across to Greenland and finally down to the Labrador coast.

We awoke next morning with the wind still howling in *Perception*'s rigging, still too strong for us to attempt the long open water passage before us. I decided to have a long-overdue clean-up and followed the stream up through the scree above the beach to where the cliffs began. I knelt down to first wash my hair. The water — snow melt from the plateau and just above the freezing point — numbed my scalp as I dipped my head in for rinsing. Perhaps that affected my judgment, because I found myself stripping off my clothes and wading into the stream to wash the rest of my body. The water stung like fire, but the pain was more than compensated for by the fact that I was clean once again after nine days of living in my survival gear. Mike soon followed me into the stream, hooting and gasping for breath. When we'd dressed, we scaled the cliffs again for another look at the birds and to get our circulation going.

We found a new observation point where, seated on a high rock, Mike was able to photograph shrill colonies of glaucous gulls and murres. The two species nested within a few meters of one another even though the gulls are predators that eat the eggs and chicks of the murres. The view from our lookout was

marvelous: to the east we could see 80 km across to the Brodeur
Peninsula and Cape York, our immediate destination. To the
north, we could see Devon Island with its many fjords and
glaciers. Below us, the ice marched with the current up Prince
Regent Inlet and sailed in on the west wind from Barrow
Strait.

It was only a few kilometers south of here, at Port Leopold on
the northeast tip of Somerset Island, that James Clark Ross's
two ships *Enterprise* and *Investigator* had been trapped in the
ice for eleven months while on a fruitless search for signs of the
Franklin expedition. An entire summer's effort had moved
them just 300 m. That was in 1848-49, by which time Franklin
had been missing for four years. During the long winter Ross
had sent out a sledge party to search along the north and west
coasts of Somerset Island, knowing that Franklin had intended,
if conditions permitted, to sail south through Peel Sound. The
sledge party traveled 800 km and endured great hardships
during the thirty-nine-day trek, in which sailors became
overworked draft animals, hauling the massive sledges favored
by the British navy for polar expeditions. Though they could
not know it, when he finally turned his exhausted and starving
men around for the long march back to their ships, Ross
and his party were only about 280 km distance from the
ice-imprisoned *Erebus* and *Terror*. Franklin was long dead but
most of his starving crew had survived until just a few months
earlier in the previous summer, when they'd set out on their
impossible journey south.

As Mike and I hiked along the cliffs toward the path that
would return us to *Perception*, the wind began to build once
more. We stopped and anxiously watched the ice drift in
around our landing place; a large mass was moving in from the
west and more was coming down from the north, threatening to
block our route across the mouth of Prince Regent Inlet. At the
foot of the cliffs, I measured the wind at 45 km/h on my pocket

anemometer. To begin a crossing with the wind this high would not be wise, but the build-up of ice before us made us wonder if this might not be our last chance. Once again we were faced with making a choice between equally unattractive options.

I decided that we would wait, and then spent the rest of the night tossing in my bivy sack, listening to the ice noisily piling in to choke the little bay where we were camped. My alarm sounded at 4 A.M. and I looked up to see the wind still lashing *Perception*'s mast-top telltale. I rolled to my right and could see that ice still blocked our escape from the bay. Setting my alarm two hours ahead, I went back to sleep. Twice more I awoke to check conditions, but it wasn't until 10:00 the next morning that wind and ice conditions had both improved enough to make a departure feasible. We radioed Resolute for a final weather update, and then checked and rechecked our survival gear and the boat's rigging, preparing for the longest open-water passage of the entire voyage.

It was just after noon when we pushed *Perception* out into the ice floes and began the crossing I had been dreading for the past three years. A lot can happen with the weather in the Arctic in the time it takes to sail 60 km of open water. Furthermore, our boat had not been designed for major open-water crossings, and we'd given ourselves an extra handicap by stuffing her with 90 kg of supplies and survival gear. We were more than a little tense as we cautiously negotiated the open leads between the ice floes cluttering the shoreline.

Wind conditions were close to ideal offshore, and we hoisted the spinnaker to take maximum advantage of our good fortune. The extra speed that gave us, however, made it even more difficult to navigate the ice pack. Working on instinct and reflex, I picked one promising lead after another, but we were being forced south into the inlet. We paused to climb a 3-m high mass of rafted ice to scout the way ahead, and the choice was obvious — there was only one lead wide enough to accommodate the boat. We followed that through the labyrinth and eventually reached an area of open water. In the distance, though, a solid band of white seemed to bar the way east. A nightmare vision of being caught out in a gale in this jungle of ice raised the hair on the back of my neck.

We found another large block of ice from which to scout our way ahead, and although there was no clear passage in any direction, there was one lead that opened to the east and looked feasible. It was closing fast, though, and we scrambled to get *Perception* underway again before the opening was sealed off. An hour later, we could see a way through the floes that would finally lead us to open water. As we left the last of the ice behind, we raised the spinnaker once again and surged ahead into the clear blue waters separating us from Cape York.

At mid-afternoon, with Prince Leopold Island still plainly visible behind us and Baffin Island just coming into view ahead, the wind stopped blowing, leaving us anxiously adrift on the slight swell of a placid sea. It was half an hour before the faintest breath of a breeze brushed our sails. Mike was lounging on the port wing reading *Adrift*, the story of Steven Callahan's seventy-six-day ordeal in the Atlantic aboard a life raft. I lay on the opposite wing with the tiller in my hand, trying to stay alert to any shift in the wind as the water trickled by our twin hulls.

An hour later the wind had picked up significantly and we were making rapid progress. But then with only 15 km to go to reach the security of Baffin Island, the wind died once again. For the next few hours, we crept along so slowly that *Perception* scarcely left a ripple in the limpid water as she glided along.

It was 10:15 P.M. when, after ten very tense hours of sailing, we finally landed on the barren shores of Baffin Island, and heartily congratulated each other on our good luck.

We quickly set up our tent and fired up the stove. Mike broke out the Canadian Club and we both had a healthy shot to toast our good fortune. Though we'd had some trouble with the ice it hadn't been insuperable, and the weather conditions had been as close to ideal as we could reasonably have hoped. All in all it had been a charmed day. We crawled into our sleeping bags at about 1:00 and were soon oblivious to the world.

"THERE'S AN OLD TRAPPER'S TALE THAT SAYS THE BEST WAY TO DEFEND YOURSELF AGAINST A POLAR BEAR ATTACK IS TO SHOOT YOUR BUDDY AND RUN LIKE HELL."

Chapter 12

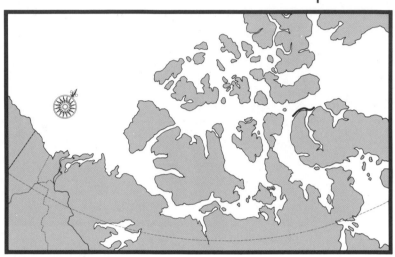

A sharp, hissing exhalation and then a heavy footfall not a meter away from our tent shocked us out of our sleep.

In a hoarse whisper, Mike told me what I already knew: *"Polar bear!"*

Trapped in our sleeping bags, we were momentarily paralyzed by fear. Then Mike shot straight up and grabbed the shotgun, flicking the safety catch off. Our ears strained for the bear's next move, but all we could hear was the sound of our hearts pounding in our chests. Bears are patient hunters and often wait quietly and patiently before attacking their prey, as they do at a seal hole. When we could stand the tension no longer, Mike cautiously unzipped the door and poked out the gun barrel. Next, he stuck his head out, just in time to see a bear that outweighed our boat. For a split second their eyes met and then the bear wheeled around and ran off. Mike dropped the gun and snatching up a camera grabbed a couple of quick shots of the fleeing animal.

"I guess he wasn't hungry," Mike observed.

I was speechless.

A thick fog was rolling in and there was virtually no wind, so we crawled back into our sleeping bags to await better sailing conditions. I surprised myself by nodding off almost immediately. When we awoke an hour later for our 9 A.M. radio schedule things were much the same; there wasn't a lot to do except wait for the wind to build. We went for a hike along the ridge behind our campsite, looking for fossils. We didn't find any, but we did find a large, round boulder that we pushed over the lip of the ridge. It gained momentum rapidly as it bounced down the rocky slope, hit the snow drift at the skirt of the beach and finally bounded into the water with a great crash and a fountain of spray. Laughing at our childish game, it felt good to release some of the recently accumulated tension.

By 2:00 there was enough wind to launch *Perception* and we tacked out into the fog and then back toward the shore, following a zigzag pattern along the coast so as not to lose touch with the land in the dense fog. As the wind continued to build, the waves grew into an irregular chop that made sailing wet and uncomfortable. The fog lifted gradually, and we could see we were approaching a stretch of coastline featuring a series of high cliffs separated by broad valleys. The effect of this topography on the wind was dramatic, to say the least. One moment we were becalmed by the cliffs; at the next valley, we'd accelerate so rapidly it would take all my concentration to keep the boat upright. Occasionally the brooding cliffs would produce not a wind shadow, but a confused and blustery maelstrom that battered us with a harsh fury. It was often impossible to guess from which direction the next gust would attack.

After six or seven hours of this, we'd had enough and pulled *Perception* ashore for the night on a beach of pebbles. I awoke with a start at about 2:30 that morning, thinking I'd heard a

bear, and went outside to investigate. The long wire that was
our radio antenna was down, but we could find neither bear nor
bear tracks. Back to bed we went, but I slept only fitfully for the
rest of the night.

In the morning we awoke to high winds and a foam-flecked
sea, and decided to explore the towering limestone cliffs behind
our campsite while we waited for the weather to improve. We
climbed to the base of a waterfall and watched as gusts of wind
blew the falling water into clouds of spray in which the sunlight
painted ever-changing rainbows. The effect of this interaction
of wind, water and sunlight was magical.

On a point of land near our campsite, I climbed a 7-m obelisk
of ice while Mike took pictures. While I was clinging to the
summit I caught a flash of white out of the corner of my eye. It
was a few hundred meters away on the ridge above the lip of the
beach and coming our way at about the speed of a walking man.
It was one of the biggest polar bears I'd ever seen – nearly half a
tonne of awesome strength and menacing beauty. We watched
through the binoculars as the animal lumbered along the ridge
toward us.

Mike decided to hike up to the ridge to get close enough for a
photograph, and since he had the gun slung over his shoulder, I
tagged along close behind. When we caught up to the bear it
was preparing for a nap, and we watched as it scraped out a
shallow depression in the spongy ground and settled in, tail to
the wind. We crept toward him slowly and carefully, but he
quickly spotted us and rose from his bed with a grunt. We were
downwind, which made him uneasy, and after observing us for
a moment he paced over to the scree slope, bounded down it
and across the beach to the sea. He loped along the water's
edge, his white coat blending with the foam, until he had placed
us upwind. It became obvious that he was heading straight for
our tent. Fearing for our supplies and equipment we raced off in
the same direction, hoping to beat him there and feeling more

than a little naked even with our gun in hand. But the bear apparently decided we were something to be feared, and he veered off toward the ocean, plunged in and began swimming out to sea with powerful strokes. We ran to the beach but he was already too far away for a decent photograph.

The following day, August 4, brought a steady downpour along with strong easterly winds and a temperature of 4°C, so we stayed cooped up in our little tent. A day spent inside a tent as tiny as ours is a long day indeed. With nothing to support your back, sitting up for any length of time begins to make your shoulders ache. So you prop yourself up on one elbow, but then that begins to hurt, too. Eventually every position you try becomes uncomfortable. It was a thoroughly depressing day. The rain fly was beginning to leak, and water was seeping through the fabric of the inner shell. We read and slept and read some more; I began *Adrift*, which put the level of our discomfort into somewhat better perspective.

We had a long way to go to Pond Inlet and not a lot of days remaining to us. In Lancaster Sound, we'd be facing open sea conditions with the potential for big swells and sustained strong winds, either of which could severely limit our progress. The most *Perception* could reasonably be expected to handle would be seas of about 4 m, and winds of 40 km/h.

The need to stretch our limbs took us outside periodically, and I noticed that throughout the day many new waterfalls had begun cascading down the rock face behind us. The stream beside our tent tripled in size and by the end of the day was busily eating away at the pebble beach, enlarging the channel to the sea. The next north wind and the waves it would bring would quickly fill the channel in again and the process of delta-making would have to begin all over.

The following morning had renewed promise; when I awoke at 6:00, the wind had moderated, though it was still from the east and right on our nose, and sea conditions looked good. At last we could get underway. But so strong was my lethargy that I crawled back into my bag for a few minutes more warmth.

By 7:30, though, my conscience had driven me out of the tent and we'd begun breaking camp. I reached Resolute on the radio, but there was no forecast available. Good. Our eyes were a better gauge, anyway.

We were on the water by 9:30, and soon found we couldn't put the starboard dagger board in place because a stone had jammed in its well. Removing these blockages was always tricky when underway; Mike leaned over the side and reached under the hull barehanded, his face a few centimeters above the water. He was finally able to dislodge the stone with our diving knife, but by that time his hand had gone completely numb and it took several minutes of shaking and rubbing to get some feeling back in his fingers.

For the first time, we were feeling the full effect of the ocean's long fetch across Baffin Bay all the way from Greenland, 700 km to the east. House-sized, steep, green swells combined with the light breeze to produce a decidedly uncomfortable motion aboard *Perception*. Mike and I were both soon feeling seasick. While Mike steered the boat, I rummaged in a waterproof bag, searching for the Sea Bands I'd brought along to try out. These are elasticized wrist bands that have a small round object about the size of a pea sewn into them. The idea is to place this bump on a tae-kwon or acupressure point between the two major tendons on the front of the wrist, three fingers above the wrist bone. This is supposed to relieve the nausea. By the time I'd located the bands in the bottom of my bag, I was feeling so ill I doubted whether anything could help. But I slipped them on, and though I didn't feel any better for wearing them, I didn't get any worse either, and managed to hang on to my breakfast. Mike had similar results.

After an hour and a half's sailing in which we covered only

about 5 km, we decided to go ashore to walk off our seasickness. The only place where the beach was not being battered by breakers was in the lee of a small point created by a melt-water stream. But as we approached this haven we spotted two polar bears — a mother and her two-year-old cub — ambling down the ridge toward our landing site. I slowed the boat thinking we might be wise to look elsewhere, but with the swells driving us ashore and our seasickness unabated, we opted to deal with the bears rather than the sea.

As we reached the surf line and jumped into the water to haul *Perception* out of the waves, the bears continued to approach our landing place, stopping now and then to browse on seaweed. They had been driven off the ice pack where they would have spent the spring season hunting seals and now, on land, they were having to forage for small mammals and birds, and I figured humans as well if the opportunity arose.

I unpacked the gun while Mike collected his cameras and began to walk straight toward the bears. I stayed behind to get a shot of Mike, the boat and the bears all in the same frame. It was a dramatic picture in the viewfinder, with Mike seated behind his tripod on the beach and the bears continuing to walk toward him. Then the animals veered inland and Mike collected his gear and pursued them, trying to get closer. Finally the mother caught our scent and really began to make tracks. With incredible ease she catapulted her 350-kg bulk across a stream, to be followed by her cub, and the two of them disappeared over a low hill. We pursued them briefly, but then decided we'd better get back to the boat and continue sailing while it was still possible.

We repositioned our Sea Bands and pushed out through the surf; I hoped we'd be able to continue moving eastward in short hops, coming ashore when necessary to walk off our seasickness. The east wind had risen, and the sea was more violent than ever. The waves had built to nearly two stories high and the crests were breaking. There was no longer any question of "borderline" conditions; it was definitely unsafe to be out there. We scanned the shoreline for a landing place, but there were only sheer cliffs and pounding surf as far ahead as we could see. There seemed to be no alternative but to return to the place we'd just left. It was more than a little tricky coming about, but as soon as we'd done so the world became a more pleasant place; the wind no longer buffeted us and roared in our ears and we were no longer engulfed in spray. It was more exciting than any roller-coaster ride as we surfed down the backs of those enormous seas with the wind at our back.

That night, when he awoke at 3 A.M., Mike saw the sun sink completely below the horizon for the first time this summer.

The east wind continued to build through the next day, August 6, making travel impossible. For much of the time it was gusting to 70 km/h and at mid-afternoon a particularly vicious blast that lifted seaweed and even stones off the beach ripped at our tent. With a sudden snap, one of the aluminum tent poles broke and drove itself through the fly.

Fearing the tear might spread under the wind's continuing onslaught, we collapsed the tent and set about trying to repair the damage in a maelstrom of blowing sand, seaweed and, now, rain. The gray duct tape we'd brought along for such emergencies wouldn't stick to the wet nylon and so Mike suggested we sew the tape over the hole. It was a task that required bare hands, and before long his fingers were aching with the cold. It took two hours for the two of us to do the job and when it was complete the patch was not a pretty sight with its five colors of thread and erratic stitching. But it seemed strong enough. We taped a splint to the broken pole and reerected the tent in the shelter of a shallow stream bed about 100 m from the boat. Once we'd weighed it down well with rocks, we slogged back to *Perception* in the pouring rain to drag her away from the crashing breakers and tied her down to a large boulder. This took some time, as we had to fasten the plastic runners under the hulls before we could get her to budge. We were in a sorry state by the time we were able to crawl back into the tent; most of our gear was wet, including both my pairs of socks, as was the tent floor.

A hot supper made us feel better, and at 9 P.M. Mike called Resolute to relay our position and check the weather forecast. He asked about the other vessels working through the passage and the operator said she had some news about *Vagabond*. The first location she mentioned was lost in static, but I heard the second quite clearly: Thule, Greenland. My heart sank — they'd beaten us through! Mike asked for confirmation and the operator now reported that *Vagabond III* was in Thule; *Vagabond II*, the passage maker, was still in her cradle in Gjoa Haven waiting for a bulldozer to be repaired so that she could be launched. So we were still in the race, and still leading. But for how much longer, I wondered, if the weather kept us pinned down on our sodden beach?

The storm continued unabated the next day, and our depression deepened. By now we'd read all the books we'd brought with us, and there was nothing to do but lie in our sleeping bags and keep warm. The next day was no better. I began to appreciate the exquisite frustration that must have been felt by the early explorers, many of whom spent months, even years locked in the ice and unable to move: John Ross, whose total forward progress in the summer of 1830 was less than a kilometer; or Franklin himself, icebound for two years in the strait named for him, his men eventually abandoning their ships in despair.

At mid-morning we spotted the two polar bears far up the beach, browsing on seaweed. Mike, determined to salvage something from this day, grabbed his cameras and the shotgun and trotted off in their direction. When he reached the stream, he removed all the clothing from his lower body and plunged into the thigh-deep, icy water. I was shivering just watching this act of photographic determination. On the far side he put his clothes back on and continued his pursuit of the animals, which were now quite nearby.

As I stood on the creek bank watching, a fog patch drifted in to obscure my vision. When it had cleared, I could see Mike crouched on the beach behind his tripod. The mother bear was walking straight toward him as he shot frame after frame. She was 15 m away now, and he was still shooting. At 10 m he exposed a few final frames and then grabbed for the shotgun.

As Mike stood up, the bear hesitated for a heart-stopping moment while it decided whether to attack or run. Then it reared up on its hind legs, spun around and fled. Mike turned slowly toward me, suppressed a war whoop and raised his arms, fists clenched in victory as the fog swirled in around him.

Around noon, the fog began to clear. The wind was still blowing from the east, but with abated fury, and it began to look as though we might actually be able to launch *Perception*. By 2:00, we'd convinced ourselves that sailing would be possible; we were by now ready to try just about anything. We broke camp and began to stow our gear aboard the boat, a process that normally took more than an hour. We had no sooner completed the entire tedious process and were about to don our survival suits when, right on cue, the wind piped up and really started to howl, gusting as high as 60 km/h.

I'd done a lot of waiting for the weather in my skiing days, but I'd never got used to it. If anything, I'd grown less patient over the years. I often felt, as I did now, that the environment had human-like motivations and was deliberately testing me. That invariably aroused in me a determination to fight back. For Mike, on the other hand, the environment just *was*, and a combative response to it seemed inappropriate.

For two hours we waited, alternately pacing up and down the

beach or seeking shelter behind the river bank, trying to keep warm. It began to rain again. The seas were building and their peaks had begun to foam. Finally it became clear we were not going to leave this place for another day, and we began the long process of unpacking our gear and setting up camp all over again, in the pouring rain and howling wind. Once again we placed the tent in the shelter of the stream bed.

For the first time, we decided to risk bringing the cookstove inside the tent, in hopes it might dry out some of our soaking clothing and equipment. We were part way through boiling water to rehydrate our dinner when a change in the sound of the little torrent beside us caused me to look outside. Our tent was all but awash in the rain-swollen creek. By the time we'd wrestled on our rain gear, the water was many centimeters deep all around us. I passed the stove out to Mike and then we moved the tent and everything in it about 15 m further away from the stream. We were now much more exposed to the wind, and at regular intervals throughout the night one or the other of us had to climb out to shift the guy lines, which we'd fastened to the biggest rocks we could find.

It was on August 9 that the weather finally permitted us to launch *Perception* into moderate seas with good visibility and a light northeast wind. All day the coastline alternated between glacier-carved valleys and spectacular cliffs surmounted by an ice cap whose dazzling whiteness indicated that the rain we'd experienced had fallen as snow on the 300 m plateau. Each valley we sailed slowly past afforded views of undulating tundra and snow-capped mountains beyond, vistas of unsurpassed beauty. We stopped only once, to walk off our incipient seasickness and nibble at trail mix, for we had hopes of sailing through the night and making the hop across Admiralty Inlet. But by midnight the wind had turned fickle and then it died, and we knew we'd have to wait for a favorable breeze before attempting the last, long, open-water passage of our voyage. We dragged *Perception* a few meters up a dry riverbed within sight of Cape Crawford, unrolled our bivy sacks on the trampoline and crawled gratefully into their warmth for the night.

In the morning the breakers were crashing in to our stretch of beach with such force that *Perception* would almost certainly have been crushed had we tried to launch. So we packed a snack, slipped on our soggy hiking boots and walked the 4 km to Cape Crawford to check sea conditions from there. The breakers on the east side of the cape were even more formidable than those at our beach; it was clear we were in for a considerable wait, once again.

Making the best of our enforced inactivity, we decided to do some more exploring, and before long we'd stumbled on an old Inuit habitation. The thick, spongy moss under our feet was littered for scores of meters in all directions with the bleached skulls, vertebrae, ribs and other bones of bowhead whales and seals. This had obviously been a good hunting area and many generations of Inuit would have enjoyed the bliss of full bellies here. Now the bones provided rich sustenance for the vegetation.

Many of the skulls appeared to be several hundred years old, but in searching the site I found a bit of evidence that this location had been used in much more recent times as well. Half-buried in the lush green moss was a small, red fire engine, badly battered but still serviceable. It was a discovery so totally unexpected that I found it strongly affecting: my heart went out to the Inuit child who had lost a prized possession.

*"MY PATIENCE WAS ALL BUT
EXHAUSTED AND I CURSED THIS OCEAN
THAT HAD TRIED TO SQUEEZE THE LIFE
OUT OF US SO MANY TIMES."*

Chapter 13

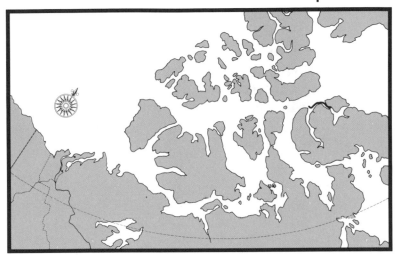

The next morning found Mike and me standing on the beach intently watching the huge breakers thunder in and smash themselves into oblivion on the shore. There was little wind, and the fog had reduced visibility to a few hundred meters.

We were counting . . . six, seven, eight . . . there seemed to be a pattern in the way the breakers arrived at the beach. A series would roll in at regular intervals and then there would be a lull before the next series arrived. If one of those immense seas were to break over *Perception* while we were trying to launch her she'd be reduced to wreckage in seconds. But what if we were to launch her during the lull between sets and then paddle like crazy to get her far enough offshore to be able to ride the incoming seas without being swept up on the beach?

Our radio schedule last night had impressed on us the need to get moving as soon as possible. We were now into the seventeenth day of the summer's voyage. In just three days, Dad and some of the sponsors would be arriving at the hamlet of Pond Inlet to greet us on our arrival at what would be the symbolic, if not the actual, completion of our expedition. And the videotape crew was getting so antsy they'd even suggested we "simulate" the conclusion of our voyage where we were, so they could shoot it and go home to their editing suite. None of them had any Arctic experience and they were evidently not enjoying themselves. Naturally Mike and I refused to have anything to do with faking the arrival or anything else and the idea, which had been only half-heartedly presented, was dropped. We had a great deal of difficulty in understanding how anyone could wish to cut short a once-in-a-lifetime opportunity to film in the Arctic we both loved so much.

We continued to watch and count. Could we do it? Mike believed we could; I was less sure. Finally a slight breeze sprang up from the northwest and with this faint encouragement I agreed to give it a try.

We pushed *Perception* into the river and walked her down toward the beach, struggling to hold her back against the strong current. At the river mouth, we positioned the boat with its bows to the waves as we stood hip deep in the torrent, Mike holding onto the starboard hull, me on the port side. The combined forces of the river current and the oncoming surf made it next to impossible for us to control the vessel, and after a few moments' struggle we withdrew back up the beach to consider again whether what we were attempting made sense. The breakers looked huge from the water's edge. One thing was certain: if we did manage to launch the boat we'd never be able to land her should anything go wrong. We'd be smashed to smithereens. The mere thought of such an accident so close to the end of our voyage made me queasy.

But we'd come too far now to turn back and after going over our battle plan once again and making sure all our equipment was in place, we pushed *Perception* back down to the sea. At the tail end of a set of 3-m breakers I yelled *"Go!"*, and in we leapt.

Mike and I leaned into the hulls and, like bobsledders at the starting gate, pushed as hard as we could down the gravel beach to the sea. We caught the water and kept pushing until we had plunged waist deep, then we dragged ourselves aboard. Immediately, we began paddling as if the hounds of hell were at our heels. Meter by agonizing meter, *Perception* moved offshore. Sweat was pouring off our bodies inside our bulky dry-suits. Ahead of us, looming gray-white through the fog, we could see a massive iceberg riding the current like the ghost of a battleship.

The next set of swells rolled toward us and then, lifting us to their crests, rolled by. They did not break over us — our timing had been good. Still we paddled furiously for fear the waves would carry us back to shore. There was no wind to fill our sails and steady the boat, and the chaotic motion soon brought seasickness. It became very difficult for me to continue paddling, and in my misery I couldn't see the sense in being out there in that mess without a breath of wind.

An interminable, stomach-wrenching hour passed before a breeze began to develop. Half paddling and half sailing, we began to make slow progress toward Cape Crawford, staying well offshore to avoid the deadly breakers. The wind continued to build and soon we were sailing eastward into the fog-shrouded waters of Admiralty Inlet, still seasick, but nonetheless in reasonably high spirits.

We were facing an open-water passage of about 50 km; at our current speed that would mean we'd be on the open ocean for three to four hours or more. The seas were already close to the limit we could safely cope with and they seemed to be coming at us from all directions. It had become very difficult to control the boat. Would the seas get any bigger? I didn't want to know.

We pulled on our Mustang flotation suits and with Mike standing on the bucking trampoline, hanging on to the mast and a stay, and me seated on the port wing, we sailed on into the fog. We were in for a wild ride.

Very quickly the cape behind us disappeared into the mists and we were fighting for survival in a sea that seemed to be boiling. There was no predicting from which direction the next waves would come, and their crests were beginning to break, keeping us bathed in a drenching spray of ice water. By now the seas were running about 5 m, with the top meter cresting as they thundered past like freight trains. The wind was gusting to 50 km/h. We hung on for dear life and it was a good thing we did; without warning a wall of water exploded over us and nearly ripped me off the stern of the boat. If I had gone overboard, there would have been no way for Mike to bring *Perception* around and rescue me in these conditions. Above the roar, Mike shouted back to me, "Hang in there. You're doing a great job!"

In spite of it all, I discovered I was having a wonderful time. In these situations of extreme stress, there is a rare intensity of focus on the task at hand. All your senses are dedicated to trying to keep the situation from becoming disastrous. It is in these moments that you feel most alive.

For two timeless hours we rode the roller coaster with our hearts in our mouths and then at last the fog began to disperse; ahead of us we could see land. With the improved visibility, we could also see for the first time the enormous size of the seas that were rolling under us. Mike furled the jib to prevent the bows from burying themselves and I told myself over and over, "Just concentrate. Don't make any mistakes. You can do it."

And then, with about 10 km of confused and angry sea separating us from land, the wind suddenly shut down completely. Without even the slight breeze she needs for steerageway, *Perception* began to wallow in the steep seas, her mast flailing and her mainsail flogging violently from side to side. The strain on the rigging was enormous and we wondered whether it could hold together. I was no longer able to keep the boat pointed in the right direction to face the oncoming seas, and the danger of capsizing became more serious than ever. We were also in danger of being dashed against the cliffs, which seemed to loom higher each minute.

Worst of all, the boat's erratic motion without the steadying effect of the wind brought back our seasickness. I looked up to see Mike leaning against the mainsail, chalk white.

"Sometimes before I throw up, I pass out," he said.

"Wonderful," I thought. "What am I supposed to do then?"

He threw up on the trampoline, and a wave sluiced it clean. He gave me a feeble grin. At least he didn't faint. I felt the familiar cold sweat rising up my back and neck, but I managed, with a struggle, to hold on to the contents of my stomach.

We had an hour of this before the wind put in another appearance and we were able to reach the eastern side of Admiralty Inlet. At the first safe landing, we pulled *Perception* ashore and stood there on the beach, weak and wobbly, but grateful for being alive.

We hadn't eaten in nearly ten hours and we were feeling very cold and weak. While the water boiled for a hot meal, we jogged and jumped along the shoreline, trying to bring some life to our frozen bodies. As always, the hot food had an almost magical rejuvenating effect and within three hours we were back on board *Perception*, running with a fresh wind from the northwest over moderate seas. The fog had rolled in once again, which meant we had to tack back in to shore periodically to determine our position, and that slowed our forward progress. But we were prepared to sail all night, if the wind held, to get to the protected waters of Navy Board Inlet before another storm developed. From there, we knew, it would be a relatively easy sail down to Pond Inlet where our welcome waited.

But it was not to be that simple; as we neared Cape Joy at about 1 A.M. the wind dropped and then quickly died. We dragged *Perception* ashore and set up camp on the beach and were asleep at 2:00.

We awoke to the chirp of my alarm at 8:00, but there was no wind, and dense fog had reduced visibility to almost nothing. As I lay in my sleeping bag, bone weary and frustrated with the unpredictable weather, it helped to recall the incredible story of how, just a few kilometers east of here, old John Ross was rescued, on August 26, 1833.

While searching for the Northwest Passage, Captain Ross and his Royal Navy crew had been seized and imprisoned by ice in the Gulf of Boothia for *four years*. They eventually abandoned their ship, trekking overland to Fury Beach on Somerset Island to retrieve a cache of naval supplies that included three whalers. They sailed in these open boats up Prince Regent Inlet and out Lancaster Sound. Hard luck had dogged them right to the end; when they'd finally spotted the sails of a ship somewhere very near where we lay, the winds were as uncooperative as they'd been for us. Despite a desperate effort to catch the vessel by rowing, the ragged, half-starved crew were not up to the challenge and the sails slipped over the horizon. The despair they must have felt can scarcely be imagined.

Four hours later another ship was sighted, and this time they were able to overtake it. The captain of the vessel couldn't believe what he was seeing: Ross and his men had been given up for dead two years earlier.

"I easily convinced him," Ross later wrote, "that what ought to have been true according to his estimate, was a somewhat premature conclusion."

The amazing thing had been that, thanks to a combination of

Ross's sterling leadership and the friendly support of local Inuit, only three of the twenty-two men who had left England with him had died during the four-year ordeal.

By about 1 P.M. most of the fog had burned off and a light breeze had sprung up from the northwest. Mike and I pushed off from the beach where we'd camped and sailed slowly along the lip of Admiralty Inlet toward Cape Joy. To the north, we could see the white glint of Devon Island's huge glaciers on the horizon. Icebergs littered the way ahead, some of them towering, cathedral-like, 20 m high.

We pulled ashore briefly to replenish our water jugs in a glacial stream and as we tacked back out into the inlet we saw a polar bear moving down the ridge where the tundra joined the beach. He splashed across the stream and then stopped suddenly where I'd been kneeling a few moments earlier filling our jugs. He'd caught our scent, and in a panic he ran down the beach and plunged into the sea.

Mike pleaded for a picture, so I turned *Perception* around and sailed toward him. But in the light to non-existent wind, he easily outdistanced us, and in any case I was not keen on the idea of playing tag with him without a decided advantage in speed. What a shot it would have made, though — the boat and the bear.

For several hours we crept along at a snail's pace, Mike and I relieving the boredom with word games and estimating the heights of icebergs. We passed Cape Joy at 5:30 and reached Cape Charles York, at the top of Admiralty Inlet, three hours later. By then we were chilled to the bone and thoroughly famished so we went ashore near a small stream to prepare supper.

Less than two hours later we were back on the water, still desperate to reach the shelter of Navy Board Inlet, now just 25 km away, before the Greenland swells returned to plague us. We had covered less than 5 km when the wind died once again and the sheer cliffs ahead made us realize that we'd better pull ashore for the night while we could. We found a small stream bed with some flat, rocky beach front and there we rolled out our bivouac sacks. Behind us the little stream trickled through a large dripping cavern it had eroded in last winter's ice.

The gentle spattering of rain on our outer Gore-Tex bags and on our faces awakened us at 5:30 on the morning of August 13. We struggled out of bed long enough to erect a makeshift shelter of our tent poles and rain fly. When we got up for good at 9:00, there was once again barely enough wind to move our Hobie through the water, and today, as we'd feared, the big swells were back, rolling all the way in from Greenland.

Our progress was excruciatingly slow as we bounced and rolled through waves of 3 m and more, both of us feeling ill from the motion. Periodically, the wind would stop blowing altogether, and we would be forced to paddle to maintain a safe distance from the shoreline, where breakers crashed against sheer gray cliffs. My patience was all but exhausted and I cursed this ocean that never seemed to give us an even break, that had tried to squeeze the life out of us so many times.

Cold, sick and hungry, we went ashore in the early afternoon to try to revive our bodies and spirits with some hot food and a little exercise. Landing safely was tricky. We had to wait for the right wave and ride it in, paddling fiercely. The instant it deposited us on land, we had to drag *Perception* out of the way of the deadly breakers that curled in behind to smash their tonnes of water on the beach. Relaunching her an hour later was no easier, and we did get caught by a breaker crashing over us as we pushed and then paddled offshore. Luckily it was one of the small ones, less than 2 m high, and it did no damage beyond drenching Mike and me, and even that didn't matter much because the two of us were by now about as miserable as we were likely to get that day.

We inched along under the influence of the fitful northeast

breeze for a couple of hours more until, once again, there was no wind at all, and we resorted to the paddles to keep ourselves safely offshore. Suddenly, and without warning, the wind resumed with a roaring vengeance and with it came a dense fog. *Perception* was now hurtling through the water, riding a fast-building sea, throwing up curtains of spray as her twin bows plunged down one wave and up the next. The sky darkened as the storm intensified and the atmosphere could only be described as hellish. I was perched on the back few inches of the port wing, one foot driven into the trampoline lacing, tiller stick in hand, and Mike sat just ahead of me, taking the brunt of the spray. There was no way we could safely land in these conditions, so we hung on and rode the backs of these white-capped chargers, our bows constantly being buried in green water, while we scanned the shoreline for a sign that it was curving south into the shelter of Navy Board Inlet.

Two hours later, and with great relief, I was able to turn *Perception* south into the inlet. But Lancaster Sound was not going to let us go without one final lesson. As we rounded the point with high cliffs to our right, the sea became hopelessly confused, the breakers seeming to explode at us from all sides. The air was full of spray and the noise was tremendous. Our boat shuddered and shook until I wondered if she'd survive.

And then we were into the inlet, rocketing along at top speed down the western shoreline. High above us on the cliffs, we caught a glimpse of a cluster of buildings we learned later were used by the Canadian government in iceberg drift studies and, it was said, submarine surveillance. We saw no submarines, either American or Soviet, but there were plenty of prowling bergs to study this day, and we were having trouble picking them out in the fog.

We struck out across the inlet in the direction of Bylot Island and an hour later its 1500-m mountain peaks were towering over us, though we could still not see the shore through the fog. At the rate we were traveling, I figured we could be all the way to the bottom of the inlet within a few hours. Hallelujah! This was more like it.

As we continued to approach Bylot Island, we could see the broad, barren, dun-colored valleys that divided the snow-crested mountains, and we marveled at the fissured gray glaciers that streamed down toward the sea. It was a place you immediately wanted to explore, though a government permit is required to do that since the island is now a vast, 11,000-square-kilometer sanctuary sheltering snow geese, murres and other sea birds.

We were gazing in awe at this spectacular scene when, as suddenly as if someone had switched off a fan, our northeast wind stopped blowing. For a few moments we were pitched violently about on the waves, unable to steer *Perception*, and then, just as suddenly, the wind began to blow furiously from the exact opposite corner of the compass. We were so thoroughly spooked by this bizarre, almost supernatural event that as soon as the wind had stabilized, we decided to land on the island, regulations or no regulations.

We came ashore at Tay Bay just in time to make our 9 P.M. radio schedule with the film crew, whom we'd last seen on Prince Leopold Island and who were now, we learned, just a few kilometers away, on the west side of the inlet. They'd traveled here from Arctic Bay on Admiralty Inlet with two Inuit guides. This was great news; we'd seen so little of them since we'd left Resolute that I had begun to wonder how they could possibly put their film together – a film that was, after all, supposed to be about our journey.

After a quick meal, we were back on the water skimming south to a rendezvous with the camera crew. At about 11 P.M. we heard the distant whine of an outboard motor, and then Mike spotted the white hull of their boat far ahead of us. As we came closer, we could see that the cinematographer's expensive video camera was finally recording the subject they'd come so far to tape — the little yellow boat. They pulled alongside and we exchanged excited greetings.

"You're here! You finally made it!" the director shouted.

Mike shouted back, "We wouldn't let you have all this fun without us!"

There was an enormous iceberg not far ahead of us and I steered for it, thinking this would provide great pictures for them, but they didn't seem much interested in following us. The light wasn't right, they said. I pointed out it was the best light we'd had all day. Then the camera stopped working altogether and they headed back to their camp. We shook our heads and agreed we'd rendezvous again next morning farther down the inlet; our plan was to sail as long as the wind held, all night if possible.

We continued our southerly course in silence, the icebergs taking on the fantastic shapes of ships and castles as we ghosted by on a breath of wind. When our fickle breeze had deserted us completely, we landed on Bylot Island and pitched our tent on the rocky beach.

Chapter 14

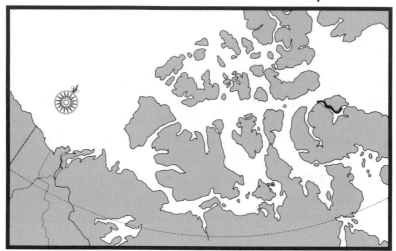

We awoke to a glorious day: bright, warm sunshine and a light
northwesterly breeze. We spoke to Pete Jess in Pond Inlet by
radio, and he told us Bill Curtsinger from National Geographic
had arrived, and they'd be flying out to see us so Bill could get
some aerial photos of *Perception*.

We launched her flying the spinnaker and made fairly good
progress down the glass-smooth waters of the inlet. To our left,
a trio of dirty-white glaciers filled three valleys, slowly carrying
millions of tonnes of ice down to the water where the bergs are
calved. I had done a lot of skiing on glaciers, but these ones
looked dangerous, with their many crevasses.

As we tacked out toward the center of the inlet in search of a
better wind, we heard the drone of an approaching aircraft, and
off to the south a tiny orange dot appeared, high over the
mountains of Bylot. I unzipped one of our red neoprene
waterproof bags and retrieved our handheld aircraft radio.

166

"This is Polar Passage calling Borek Air. How do you read? Over."

On the third try the reply came. "Jeff, we read you loud and clear."

It was Pete, and with him was Bill Curtsinger, his suitcase full of cameras. There were a dozen other passengers, including several corporate executives who had arrived in Pond Inlet with my father to see a little of the Arctic and if possible be present at our arrival. For the next half hour they flew by us from every conceivable angle, making a dozen or more passes. Sometimes they swept so low we were choking in engine exhaust. The racket was deafening.

When they'd finished, they flew off to the west in hope of being able to drop off some fuel and other supplies ordered by the video team and their Inuit guides on the west side of the inlet. But in the end they were unable to find a safe place to land the Twin Otter and returned to Pond Inlet with the supplies still on board.

It wasn't until mid-afternoon that the video team got into gear; we knew that they were running short of fuel, but far more serious for them was the fact that they'd run out of sugar and cigarettes for their guides, Moses and his ancient father. This was not a happy group.

When they caught up with us, the cameraman taped us skimming along through a fleet of icebergs against a background of some of the most spectacular scenery of the voyage: the stark, ice-scoured plateau of Baffin Island on one side and the peaks and glaciers of Bylot Island on the other. By now it was so warm Mike and I weren't even wearing gloves. The sea sparkled gaily as the sunlight was reflected by a million tiny wavelets.

The cameraman came aboard with his $60,000 video camera and taped Mike and me from a score of different angles as we coaxed *Perception* along over the glassy sea. This was all laudable and necessary, but I couldn't help thinking that these images, the only ones of their kind, were going make the whole trip seem like a holiday at Club Med. Was this the Arctic teaching me another lesson in humility?

When we all pulled into a beach briefly for a conference, Mike and I had our first chance to meet Moses and his father. Moses spoke English fairly well, but his father understood hardly a word. They were naturally anxious to get back to their families at Arctic Bay as soon as possible. The lack of sugar and cigarettes wasn't helping their morale; neither was the fact that they were both hungry. They didn't like the freeze-dried food the video team supplied, and it had been many days since they'd killed a seal.

The director was of course sympathetic to their plight — far too sympathetic, I thought. He was ready to return immediately to Pond Inlet from where the guides could start their journey home — even though that would mean sacrificing the only real opportunity he would have to tape *Perception* under sail. I found the idea outrageous, but I did my best to keep my feelings under control. At lunch we tried to humor the Inuits' taste buds with some Gatorade in the tea in lieu of sugar, but this was only a qualified success. I tried my best to breathe some enthusiasm back into the video team. But I guess they'd just spent too much time struggling with the frustrations of this sometimes frightening land. We finally convinced the crew to stay with us until we set up camp for the night — if the wind held, I intended to make sure that wouldn't be for a good many more hours.

There was no wind at all at that moment, but Mike and I were eager to show some leadership and spirit so we launched *Perception* anyway and began paddling. Before long the northeasterly picked up and we raised the chute and tacked out toward the center of the inlet where the wind was stronger. We were flying along now in near-perfect conditions and I had visions of being in Pond Inlet the following morning if the wind held.

Ahead of us was a vast and wonderful crenelated iceberg the size of a small castle, and in the magical evening light it took on a luminescence that was simply breathtaking. Where, we wondered, was the video team? This was without a doubt the single most stunning image of the entire voyage and Mike desperately wanted to be able to shoot *Perception* and the berg from their boat — here was a potential *National Geographic* cover shot.

We sailed completely past this fortress of ice. So enormous was it that it affected the wind patterns and we had a lot of trouble controlling the spinnaker, at one point dropping it in the water. The sea boiled around its base as it drifted in the current and from time to time huge chunks of ice would break off with a groan and a snap and crash into the sea. We briefly considered inflating the Sea Seat so Mike could get his photographs, but the micro-environment created by the berg was so dynamic and unpredictable that we decided it would be unsafe.

We sailed several kilometers farther down the inlet before the video crew caught up with us. As they pulled alongside, I couldn't help venting my frustration.

"You missed the best filming opportunity of the entire journey," I yelled above the racket of their engine. There was no response. The boat simply pulled away and headed south on a course for Pond Inlet, leaving us to bob in its wake.

At about 10 P.M. we were drifting along in very light winds, nibbling on trail mix and chocolate bars when it suddenly occurred to me that today was Mike's birthday. I congratulated him — he'd forgotten, too. It was hard to believe that this was the third birthday he'd had on this voyage: the first on Burrow Island in 1986; the next year's among the Royal Geographical Islands; and now today's.

Around midnight it started to rain and the wind began to gather force. Within twenty minutes we were being lashed by sleet driven by 50 km/h winds from the east. For a while we were able to press on – I was anxious to get to Pond Inlet while the corporate sponsors were still there and before the video crew went south. But as the storm intensified, we were forced to head for shore, where we pulled the boat up on a sandy beach and waited for the wind to abate. I pleaded silently for the elements to cooperate long enough to let us reach Pond Inlet, but of course the wind only got stronger and at 2:00 in the morning we put up our tent and crawled in for the night.

The next day, August 15, was the twenty-first day of this final leg of the voyage, from Cape Anne to Baffin Bay. Outside our tent the conditions were not encouraging. It was raining, and there was a blustery wind from the east, which meant that as soon as we rounded the corner into Eclipse Sound and Pond Inlet we'd have 80 km of hard slogging through choppy seas into a headwind. Then we'd have to cross 25 km of open water to get to the village of Pond Inlet on the south side of the inlet itself.

By the time we'd broken camp we were cold, wet and weary. Our strategy was to sail offshore into the teeth of the weather until the waves became big enough to stifle our forward motion, and then tack back toward shore. These were just about the worst possible conditions for catamaran sailing and our progress was painfully slow; worse, the strain on the rigging and the struts that held our little vessel together was enormous. Given the torture she'd already endured, we were by no means certain she could take much more.

We didn't think *we* could take much more by mid-afternoon and went ashore to have some food and to try to get the blood circulating in our numbed arms and legs. We ate, walking aimlessly on the beach, limbering our bodies, trying not to think of what the rest of the day had in store for us. As much as we dreaded going on in these conditions, we knew that if we waited for the weather to improve, the odds were that it would get worse.

As we were preparing to push *Perception* back into the waves, Mike challenged me to a game. The rules were simple: the players bend over at the waist and spin around eight times, then run to a spot 15 m away and return. The first one back wins.

Okay, I thought. No problem.

When Mike said "Go!", I spun around as fast as I could. Then I straightened my body and charged forward. Or so I thought — I was actually staggering sideways and before I'd covered 3 m, I crashed to the ground. For a moment, I couldn't get up, and when I did Mike was wobbling toward the turnaround point. Rather than let him win I threw a clumsy tackle at his legs and we hit the sand in a heap, laughing hysterically. We finally departed, leaving on the virgin sand of that deserted beach a set of footprints that Sherlock Holmes himself couldn't have deciphered.

We continued to tack east up Eclipse Sound, hugging the shoreline of Bylot Island and hoping every moment for a break in the weather that would let us dash across to the shore of Baffin Island. Four hours later, when our break hadn't come we decided, as we had so many times before, to make the dash anyway. Conditions, if horrible, were at least relatively stable, and I thought we could just make it. In any case, it would certainly be a dramatic way to reach the village, blasting into the little harbor in this kind of weather.

As we turned south toward open water, an airplane swooped down through the cloud cover and banked into a tight circle overhead before flying off in the direction of Pond Inlet. Drenched in windblown spray, and with *Perception* bucking like a bronco, we were unable to retrieve our aircraft radio to make contact, but I learned later that the plane had been carrying Dad and the group back to Pond Inlet from some Arctic char fishing.

Soon we were at the halfway point of the open water crossing — the point of no return — and I have seldom felt more acutely vulnerable. We were so tantalizingly close to our destination and yet I could not believe the Arctic was going to let us have our victory.

The crossing took two hours, and as we neared the southern shore the wind turned fluky and then swung north. Now I found myself begging the wind to keep blowing.

"Don't die," I repeated over and over again. But at 9:30, die it did, leaving us becalmed 8 km away from the village. This was to be the last lesson in humility. Instead of sailing in triumphantly to meet our little welcoming party, we were going to have to arrive ignominiously under paddle power. We unshipped the paddles and got to work without a word.

A motor launch appeared on the horizon racing toward us. As it came near I could see Dad, the video crew and Bill Curtsinger from National Geographic on board. Dad pulled out a bottle of champagne and held it high in the air; while the camera rolled he passed it to me, grinning from ear to ear. I began to realize that we'd actually made it — almost.

We still had an hour's paddling to do to get to Pond Inlet. I was tempted to open the bottle right away, but I knew that would only slow us down, so we got back to work. We shouted back and forth to our chase boat, with Mike and me talking excitedly; I found it impossible to adequately express my gratitude to him for weathering three summers aboard the boat with me. We hadn't always seen eye to eye, but over the seasons my respect for his unique strengths and talents had grown enormously.

I was having difficulty understanding my own oddly subdued emotions as we paddled on. I knew of course that this was just the symbolic ending to our expedition; that we still had

60 km to cover before we'd arrive at the official passage terminus in Baffin Bay. I began to realize, too, that it is the voyage and not its conclusion that provides most of the satisfaction. An expedition is like a parallel life. You conceive the idea, and it gestates within you and takes on a form. When it is born and becomes a reality you are tested, and you learn and grow with the experience. The voyage challenges, troubles and tries to destroy you. You draw on reserves you never knew existed within you. In doing so you pull and stretch yourself into adulthood. When the expedition ends, its life over, the post-mortem eulogies begin: the books, the movies, the public appearances, the thank-yous.

For me, this was a time of uncertainty and sadness, and I knew I was going to need to generate new ideas and dream new dreams.

On we paddled, the bottle of chilled champagne providing an increasing temptation. When we couldn't wait any longer, I popped the cork. Dad pulled alongside and handed us a silver goblet I recognized as one that had played a part in family celebrations many times in the past. Mike and I filled it to the brim and drank victoriously. How glorious it tasted! I offered some to the other boat, but they insisted we drink it all, and we did.

As we neared the town, the film crew asked us to paddle around a huge iceberg that was grounded outside the harbor. We did that and paddled on to the outer fringes of the settlement. The town had spread out since I'd last been here in 1975. I was twelve then and had come with Dad on an expedition to take the first underwater photographs of the narwhal. Bill Curtsinger had been there, shooting pictures for *National Geographic*, and now he was standing on the beach with his camera aimed at *Perception*. Behind him were a clutch of our sponsors, including Peter Widdrington, Norman James, Roger Lindsay and many other friends. Even though it was now

10:30 at night, a sizeable portion of the town's population had turned out as well. Then Mike and I took the last few strokes and we were there.

A hoard of kids descended on us; I heard myself saying in jest, "Where are we?"

I splashed ashore and hugged Dad, and then Mike and Pete Jess and there were smiles and handshakes and more hugs . . . it's a blurry memory.

When we'd been introduced to the mayor of Pond Inlet and many others, we dragged *Perception* up on the beach and loaded our gear into a pickup that bounced us up a dusty street past colorfully painted bungalows and the bright orange school, up the hill to the town's cosy hotel.

There, the first order of business was to have a shower, my first in more than three weeks. Mike went off to look for his mother. Then it was more champagne in the sitting room. I kept hugging and thanking Dad and Pete Jess, who had traveled so far with me to help fulfill this dream. At 2 A.M. I dragged my bivy sack out behind the hotel and slept there on a wooden platform with Dad and four or five others whom the hotel was too cramped to accommodate.

Chapter 15

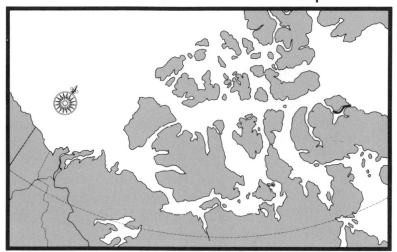

The party was over, literally and figuratively, when my father and his group boarded their plane at noon the next day to continue their Arctic explorations.

Suiting up in survival gear and getting back aboard *Perception* was about the last thing in the world I felt like doing, but there was no way out of it. The video crew would be gone in two days, and the only way to get *Perception* out of the Arctic was aboard the sea-lift vessel that was now unloading at Pond Inlet and that would be departing in two days as well.

We stalled for as long as we could, waiting for some wind, Finally at 8 p.m. we departed on the merest breath of a breeze, sailing slowly, slowly away from Pond Inlet and the group of well-wishers on the beach before resorting to the paddles. By then, I suspect, even Mike was growing frustrated with the lack of cooperation we'd been getting from the elements. The idea of having to paddle the entire 60 km to Button Point didn't bear considering; we took it one stroke at a time and tried to keep the thought out of our minds.

After about an hour's effort, we gave up in disgust and tried lining *Perception* along the shore. At least that way there would be the sensation of making progress. We attached 15-m lines to the bow and stern of the inshore hull and set off on foot, towing the boat. As we trudged along, we passed a bottle of navy rum back and forth.

Initially the walking was easy, but more and more rocks appeared on the shoreline and after an hour or so we were back aboard the boat. We could still see the village in the distance behind us. About the only thing our exertions were doing was keeping us warm.

The frustration of our slow progress was more than compensated for by the beauty of our surroundings – the majestic mountain peaks and ancient glaciers of Bylot Island and the barren coastal plateau of Baffin Island with blue-gray mountains brooding in the background. Ahead, where the Baffin Island mountains reached the sea, Mt. Herodier, a bald, dome-shaped peak, was decorated in a brilliant rainbow for much of the evening. Huge, blue-white icebergs glided serenely down the inlet on the current, beckoning us onward.

About midnight a cat's-paw of wind crept across the surface of the water, filling *Perception*'s sails and allowing Mike and me to rest. On shore a pair of nineteenth-century whalers' tombs came into view with their weathered wooden markers. A light rain had begun, and in the twilight mist the graves took on a surreal quality that was powerfully moving. What terrors, I wondered, had these men suffered in this harsh environment? We went ashore briefly to stand at the grave site, and I said a silent prayer for them – two young Danes perhaps not unlike us, so very far from home.

We both felt thoroughly chilled when we returned to *Perception*, so we put on extra layers of underwear before donning our dry-suits. In the unlikely event that the wind held, we planned to sail right through the night.

The wind not only held, it continued to build and I steered a course across the inlet toward the easternmost corner of Bylot Island. We were really moving now, as I kept driving *Perception* deeper downwind, pushing her to her maximum performance, reveling in the speed. Ahead of us was the open expanse of Baffin Bay, with Greenland 700 km over the horizon.

We sped along the southern shoreline of Bylot Island straining to find Button Point. Could we get there before the wind and waves forced us to stop?

With the wind peaking at 55 to 60 km/h, we furled the jib and continued under mainsail alone. The crests were being blown off the waves. We'd now been awake more than twenty hours, and I had to keep reminding myself, "Keep concentrating. Don't slip up. You can do it."

The sun burst out from behind the mountains, a blazing orange ball hanging directly in our path just above the horizon. As if to make amends for her earlier truculence, Nature seemed to be pulling out all the stops to provide us with a dramatic setting for the completion of the voyage.

Our formal and very public finish at Pond Inlet had seemed artificial and unsatisfying, not because it wasn't the true geographical finish line, but because our contest had been a private one, between us and Nature. Nature had tested us and permitted us a personal triumph that had nothing to do with other men, nor with victory or defeat in the way that people normally define them. She had permitted us to survive and grow and learn in her arms, and in a sense, and if only for this moment, to become one with her.

There, suddenly, was the lonely Thule Inuit ruin that marks Button Point, its low stone and whalebone walls just visible against the sun's glare. It was 5:08 A.M. on the morning of the one-hundredth day of our voyage as we flashed by into Baffin

Bay, the spray from our twin hulls making rainbows in the sun,
completing history's first sail-powered transit of the Northwest
Passage — a 400-year-old dream.

* * *

*August 17th, 1988, 6:50 A.M. I sit here at Button Point snug in the
ruins of a Thule Inuit hut that is at least 400 years old: as old, in
fact, as the dream of sailing the Northwest Passage. A four-foot
wall of rock and whalebone protects me from the howling wind.
The wall next to me is supported by a 100-kg bowhead whale skull,
its powder-white surface cracked and crevassed by time. Orange
lichen which takes more than a century to grow is creeping over its
surface.*

*The room is about 5 m square, and I am sitting on the sleeping
platform that runs around the perimeter, writing with bare hands,
a luxury not often permitted me on this voyage. I've been up for
nearly twenty-three hours now, but cannot sleep. The joy and
excitement are too great.*

*My thoughts go out to the people that lent their ideas, time, and
support to making this expedition work.*

*Perception rests on the rocky beach, the wind whistling in her
rigging, her bright yellow hulls radiant in the morning sunlight.
She was, as I'd hoped, the ideal vessel for this voyage. In light airs
she glides along swiftly and in storms she is stable, though
frighteningly wet, and she can be easily beached when the going
gets too tough. When ice is an obstacle, she can, with some
considerable effort, be hauled up and over by her crew.*

*In fact she is the embodiment of the watchword to survival in the
Arctic adaptability.*

*This seems the finest place in the world to be. I am totally
happy.*

HISTORICAL HIGHLIGHTS OF THE
EXPLORATION OF THE NORTHWEST PASSAGE

1576	Frobisher's first voyage in search of the Northwest Passage.
1585-1587	Davis searches the shores of Labrador and Baffin Island for the Passage.
1610	Hudson sails into Hudson Bay and is abandoned there by his crew.
1616	Bylot and Baffin sail into the northern reaches of Baffin Bay.
1818	Ross sails as far as Lancaster Sound but turns back at its entrance.
1819-1820	Parry makes his classic voyage into Lancaster Sound — over 800 km — and spends the winter at Melville Island.
1819-1820	Franklin's first expedition to the arctic coast via the Coppermine River.
1825-1827	Franklin's second expedition to the arctic coast via the Mackenzie River.
1829-1833	Ross sails into the central Arctic.
1845-1848	Franklin's ill-fated voyage in *Erebus* and *Terror*.
1848	Plans made to rescue Franklin — Sir James Ross fails to find any traces.
1848-1850	Many expeditions — overland and by sea — including those of Austin, Richardson, Pullen, M'Clure and Collinsen, fail to find Franklin or his ships.
1852	Belcher sails with five ships including the *North Star* to search the central Arctic for Franklin. *North Star* is anchored off Beechey Island.
1850-1854	M'Clure's ship wrecked — survivors walk to Beechey Island and are the first men to cross the Northwest Passage.
1853	The *Breadalbane* sinks off Beechey Island.
1854	Rae finds traces of the Franklin expedition.
1857-1859	M'Clintock finds more traces of the Franklin expedition.
1903-1906	Amundsen's *Gjoa* is the first ship to motor-sail through the Northwest Passage.
1940-1944	The Royal Canadian Mounted Police auxiliary schooner *St. Roch* completes the Passage. It is the first to do it from west to east, and the first to navigate it both ways.
1969	The *Manhattan* is the first commercial vessel to negotiate the passage.
1983	The *Breadalbane* is discovered by an underwater research team lead by Dr. Joe MacInnis.
1986-1988	The *Perception* is the first to sail across the Northwest Passage, completing a 400-year-old dream.

INDEX

ABOUT THE AUTHOR

JEFF MACINNIS
THE HISTORIC FIRST SAIL THROUGH THE NORTHWEST PASSAGE. IF YOU CAN DREAM IT ... YOU CAN DO IT ...

Polar Passage is a story about the Arctic, it's unusual beauty, historical highlights and challenges. It is also a story of 100 days of numbing cold, sleepless nights, face to face encounters with polar bears and moments when the expedition's small 18-foot boat was almost crushed by ice.

Polar Passage is presented by Jeff MacInnis, the leader of the first expedition to sail the 4000-kilometer Northwest Passage – a goal that has eluded explorers for four centuries. The passage has claimed more lives than Mt. Everest.

MacInnis, a graduate from the University of Western Ontario Business School, raised the $200,000 needed for his unique venture. The expedition tested technology and techniques in the Arctic for a number of North American corporations.

MacInnis has appeared on Canadian television programs including a one-hour CBC *Polar Passage* special, *Front Page Challenge, Fifth Estate, Canada AM,* and *The Journal.* He is the author of several magazine articles including a feature in *National Geographic.* He has lectured in Canada and the United States to organizations such as IBM, Merrill Lynch and Motorola.

"Your determination, perseverance and commitment to excel in the face of tremendous challenges represent the finest example of the true potential in us all. Indeed, we are better people by having had the opportunity of being exposed to your shining evidence of excellence in the pursuit of a dream." Merrill Lynch

For further information please contact: Jeff MacInnis 914 Yonge St., Suite 1605, Toronto, Ontario M4W 3C8